"

Orange Shirt Day began in 2013. I've always wanted to tell the story of how Orange Shirt Day started and to acknowledge the people who were involved in its creation. Thank you to everyone who continues to participate in Orange Shirt Day across Canada and beyond.

I didn't just get out of bed one day and decide that September 30th would be Orange Shirt Day. There is a story behind it, a long line of events that took place and people who contributed to making the day what it is today. Through this book I have the chance to tell my story and thank the people who have helped to create this movement.

Thank you for taking the time to read this book. I hope it will fill in some of the gaps to help you understand what Orange Shirt Day is all about; why the colour orange, why we chose the slogan "Every Child Matters", and the need to honour Residential School Survivors, their families, and to remember those children who didn't come home.
With respect and in friendship,

"

Phyllis Webstad

2023 Official Orange Shirt
Designed by Charliss Santos

Traditional Territory Acknowledgment

Medicine Wheel Publishing and the Orange Shirt Society acknowledge that this book was developed on the traditional territories of the Coast Salish peoples including the Sc'ianew people, the Lekwungen people, the T'Sou-ke people as well as on the traditional territories of the Interior Salish people, the Secwépemc (Shuswap), including the T'exelcemc First Nation (Williams Lake Indian Band) and the Xatśūll First Nation (Soda Creek Indian Band).

Thank you

The Orange Shirt Society would like to thank all the wonderful people who, because of their sacrifice of time and energy, led to the creation of Orange Shirt Day and the Orange Shirt Society.

Without you, this movement would not be possible. Whether you were an artist, volunteer, Chief, government official, participant, sponsor, student, teacher, Survivor, member of a Survivor's family, current or past board member of the Orange Shirt Society or any other future participant, we would like to thank each of you for your contribution in making Orange Shirt Day what it is today.

TABLE OF CONTENTS

Beaded orange shirts for the Prince George Native Friendship Center. The artists include Jean Baptiste, Lynette La Fontaine, Shalane Pauls and Nicole Evanoff.

CHAPTER 1

INTRODUCTION & THE VISION
THAT INSPIRED ORANGE SHIRT DAY

Welcome. Kukwstsetsélp (Thank you to all) for your courage and for opening your heart to learning, growing and striving to make our country more inclusive and unified. By reading Orange Shirt Day, you are embarking on an important journey to increase your knowledge and understanding of the significance of Orange Shirt Day, the Orange Shirt Society, Canada's shameful history of Indian Residential schools and their impacts, **Indian Residential School Reconciliation** and how to participate in a **National Day for Truth and Reconciliation**.

The only way to achieve Indian Residential School reconciliation is to acknowledge the true history and learn from it, no matter how difficult. The Orange Shirt Society hopes this book will help you to feel confident and empowered to continue to work towards Indian Residential School reconciliation regardless of your age, background and position in life. Everyone has a part to play. This book will offer you knowledge, skills and the opportunity to start the process of reconciling what took place in the Residential Schools, while also gaining a deeper understanding of the ongoing mistreatment of Indigenous Peoples.

As you begin your journey in understanding Orange Shirt Day and reconciliation, we ask that you pay close attention to your heart, mind and feelings. If you feel sad or troubled while reading this book, please take a break and talk to a parent, teacher, or adult you trust about what you are feeling.

Indian Residential School Reconciliation is an ongoing collective process that involves both Indigenous and non-Indigenous Canadians bravely acknowledging, and educating each other, on the mistreatment of Indigenous peoples through the Residential School System. Reconciliation aims to create a new legacy for Indigenous Canadians that supports a healing journey and sees a respectful resurgence of cultural traditions.

National Day for Truth and Reconciliation "Each year, September 30 marks the National Day for Truth and Reconciliation. The day honours the children who never returned home and Survivors of Residential Schools, as well as their families and communities. Public commemoration of the tragic and painful history and ongoing impacts of residential schools is a vital component of the reconciliation process." [1] The day is considered a national federal statutory holiday.

CANADA BASED TOLL-FREE HELP LINES

- 24-hour National Indian Residential School crisis line at 1-866-925-4419
- Indigenous Hope for Wellness Helpline 1-855-242-3310
- Kids Help Phone at 1-800-668-6868
- Suicide Prevention and Support at 1-833-456-4566
- 9-1-1 Emergency

This book was created to educate you on the Orange Shirt Day movement, Indian Residential School history and the process of reconciliation. There is something for everyone within these pages and it is our hope that you use this text as a guideline to forge meaningful and purposeful relationships that have the potential to pave a way towards reconciliation. The Orange Shirt Society invites teachers, government officials, parents and other influential people to use this text as an educational tool and offer this knowledge to the younger generations who are forging new paths for a bright future.

TERMINOLOGY USED IN THIS BOOK

Indian is an erroneous and outdated term used to describe Indigenous people. It is based on the mistaken assumption by early European explorers that they had arrived in India. Unfortunately, it is still a *'legal'* term employed within the 1876 Indian Act, which is still in use. Today *'Indian'* is a derogatory term, and it will only be used in this book when referring to Indian Residential Schools and other legal terms within the Indian Act.[2]

Indigenous, or **Aboriginal**, people, *"are the descendants of the original inhabitants of North America. The Canadian Constitution recognizes three groups of Aboriginal people - Indians, Métis and Inuit. These are three separate peoples with unique heritages, languages, cultural practices and spiritual beliefs."* [3]

First Nations *"is a term used to describe Aboriginal peoples of Canada who are ethnically neither Métis nor Inuit."* [4]

Inuit *"Aboriginal people in Northern Canada, who live in Nunavut, Northwest Territories, Northern Quebec and Northern Labrador. The word means 'people' in the Inuit language —Inuktitut. The singular of Inuit is Inuk."* [5]

Métis *"means a person who self-identifies as Métis, is distinct from other Aboriginal peoples, is of historic Métis Nation Ancestry and who is accepted by the Métis Nation."* [6]

WHAT THIS BOOK EXPLORES

Orange Shirt Day, September 30th, is a day to honour Residential School Survivors, their families, and remember those **children who didn't come home**. This book will provide you with an opportunity to understand the power and significance of reconciliation in regards to Orange Shirt Day. It is everyone's responsibility to understand the continuing impacts connected to this **National trauma** and how we all, as people of varying backgrounds, ancestry and age, can ensure Residential Schools never happen again. In order to embrace reconciliation and change all of us, both Indigenous and non-Indigenous, must come together to promote the healing and acknowledgment of this tragic time in Canadian history. Everyone must work together for a better and inclusive future in which EVERY CHILD MATTERS.

Chief Willie Sellars, Elder Millie Emile, Elder Virginia Gilbert and Phyllis Webstad at the 2019 Williams Lake Orange Shirt Day. Photo is by Monica Lamb-Yorski of the Williams Lake Tribune.

A **National trauma** occurs when a traumatic event or experience affects a collective group of people across a country. Indian Residential Schools have resulted in a national trauma.

The City of **Williams Lake** lies within the Cariboo Regional District of British Columbia and is situated on the traditional territory of the T'exelcemc (Williams Lake First Nation), who are members of the Secwépemc Nation (Shuswap People).[7]

Children who didn't come home from Residential Schools because they died, from malnutrition, disease or injuries due to the circumstances and abuses endured at the schools. Many children also attempted to run away from the Residential Schools, but they died trying to find their way home. Records show that 6000 children died in Residential Schools, but the records are incomplete and it is believed that far more children didn't come home. There are ongoing investigations pertaining to the finding of unmarked and undocumented graves and burial sites at Residential School sites across Canada.[8]

THE BOOK AT A GLANCE

This book offers an opportunity to engage within yourself and beyond to learn about the skills, attitudes and relationships required to walk a path towards Reconciliation. In order to achieve this important purpose, this book will offer you the following:

- A brief history of the events leading to the implementation of Residential Schools
- A brief history of Residential Schools in Canada, focusing on the impacts of St. Joseph's Mission Residential School in **Williams Lake**, B.C.
- The brief overview of the St. Joseph's Mission Residential School Commemoration Project started a vision of reconciliation that led to Orange Shirt Day
- The creation and movement of Orange Shirt Day and the Orange Shirt Society
- How to participate in Orange Shirt Day respectfully, authentically and effectively
- Reflections on Reconciliation

This book will feature student art projects inspired by Orange Shirt Day. These art pieces are reflections of the thought processes of students across Canada in response to the Orange Shirt Day movement. The Orange Shirt Society sincerely thanks the hundreds of brilliant students and teachers who kindly submitted their artwork. Although not every art piece could be included, the Orange Shirt Society is humbled by the amazing and creative responses.

Terms that require a definition will be shown in **bold font**. For these terms, there will be a definition provided at the bottom of the text and/or in the back of the book in the glossary.

To engage with this book effectively as a teacher, there is an educational curriculum-based study guide designed to give additional tools and resources specialized for the classroom. For more information please find the Orange Shirt Day: September 30th Study guide available at **www.medicinewheelpublishing.com**

For more Orange Shirt Day resources visit **www.orangeshirtsociety.org**

Photo is by Jacqueline Maurer. These orange medicine pouches were crafted by the Dze L K'ant Friendship Centre on the Wet'suwet'en Territory.

THE VISION THAT INSPIRED ORANGE SHIRT DAY

Orange Shirt Day is September 30th, which is recognized annually on the same day as Canada's federal statutory holiday — the National Day for Truth and Reconciliation. Orange Shirt Day is a legacy of the St. Joseph's Mission Residential School Commemoration Project held in Williams Lake, B.C., in May of 2013. That week-long commemoration project was inspired by **Chief Fred Robbins**, who is Northern Secwépemc (Shuswap) from Esk'etemc First Nation (Alkali Lake).[9] Chief Fred Robbins had a vision for reconciliation which involved all people remembering and learning what happened at St. Joseph's Mission Residential School, honouring and helping the Survivors to recover from their experiences and ultimately reconciling together.

Chief Fred Robbins' vision was to create positive long-lasting change and harmony among Indigenous and non-Indigenous peoples within Williams Lake and throughout the Cariboo Region. In order to achieve this, he needed to involve the entire community in understanding and learning what happened in that Residential School just down the road, before any healing and reconciliation could take place. In his efforts to bring people together, he invited Chiefs, Councils, local and provincial elected officials, RCMP officers, schools and churches, as well as Indigenous and non-Indigenous local residents to a series of community-building events.

CHIEF FRED ROBBINS

*Every Child Matters. It's that next generation that we have to start teaching... We need to start creating a new legacy, and it starts within the communities... The people need to start coming together... **Everything that ever happened to First Nations people across Canada started with these schools**. Physical, sexual, mental, discrimination, genocide, treason, everything started with these schools. **And to move forward we need to recognize that and that's why we are here today.** Let's recognize that together as a people, not as First Nations and non-First Nations but as a people... that's how we have to do this.*

- Chief Fred Robbins, Esk'etemc First Nation, May 17, 2013. [10]

Truth and Reconciliation
Commission of Canada

The Truth and Reconciliation Commission of Canada (TRC) was founded on June 2, 2008 and aimed to reveal the truths of Residential Schools and provide support for Survivors and their families. The TRC was created out of the Indian Residential School Settlement Agreement (IRSSA), which was announced in 2006. The IRSSA was an agreement between both the Government of Canada and Residential School Survivors. This agreement was reached to settle a class action lawsuit by Indian Residential School Survivors. It required that the Government of Canada issue an official apology and provide a compensation package of nearly two billion dollars that was paid out to Survivors.[11] At the time, it was recognized as the largest class action suit in Canadian history.

As a result of this historic settlement agreement, the TRC was created and the Government of Canada issued an official apology for its role in creating government-sponsored Residential Schools. On June 11, 2008, just days after the birth of the TRC, Prime Minister Stephen Harper stood in the House of Commons and issued an apology on behalf of Canada to all Residential School Survivors. [12]

Between 2008 and 2015, the TRC revealed the dark truths of Residential Schools and provided a platform for Indigenous peoples to be heard and begin their journey of reconciliation.

In order to effectively participate in the ongoing process of reconciliation, in its conclusion in 2015, the TRC offered 94 calls to action. The calls to action provide concrete steps on an array of reconciliation topics including education, child welfare, language and culture, health, and professional development. [13]

In 2013, the TRC travelled to Williams Lake to participate in the St. Joseph's Mission Commemoration Project events which were inspired by Chief Fred Robbins' vision for reconciliation. The TRC Chair, Chief Justice Murray Sinclair, who is now a Canadian Senator, participated in and chaired the events. The series of events included the unveiling of memorial monuments, a youth video project, educational opportunities, Survivor statement gathering and a reunion for Survivors. It was at these events that Phyllis Webstad shared the story of her orange shirt resulting in the international movement Orange Shirt Day. [14]

(Chief) Fred Robbins is Northern Secwépemc (Shuswap) from Esk'etemc First Nation (Alkali Lake). Chief Fred Robbins had a vision for reconciliation which involved all people remembering and learning what happened at St. Joseph's Mission Residential School, honouring and helping the Survivors recover from their experience and ultimately reconciling together.

PHYLLIS (JACK) WEBSTAD'S STORY

Phyllis Webstad photographed by Danielle Shack of DS Photography

A teepee set up for Orange Shirt Day 2015 in Calling Lake, Alberta. Photo taken by Angela Lightning.

Beadwork and photo by Kristin Spray.

In 2013, Residential School Survivor **Phyllis Webstad** was asked to speak at a press conference promoting reconciliation events in her community. Phyllis courageously shared her personal and traumatic experience. [15] Orange Shirt Day was born out of that speech. Phyllis Webstad works as an ambassador for the Orange Shirt Society and continues to share her story in hopes of inspiring many people to walk toward truth and reconciliation. The influential efforts of Chief Fred Robbins, and later Phyllis Webstad, as well as many other people's efforts, led to the Orange Shirt Day movement. Now, Orange Shirt Day passionately spreads the message that "Every Child Matters."

Phyllis Webstad is Northern Secwépmc from Stswecem'c Xget'tem First Nation, (Canoe Creek/Dog Creek Indian Band). When she was just six-years-old in 1973, she went to Residential School for the first time. On her first day at St. Joseph's Mission Residential School, near Williams Lake, B.C., she wore her brand new shiny orange shirt, bought for her by her Granny. Phyllis was so excited to go to school and wear her new shirt, but when she arrived her orange shirt was taken away, never to be worn again. She survived the Mission for 300 sleeps.

The orange shirt has now become a symbol of hope and reconciliation. To Phyllis, the colour orange has always symbolized that she did not matter. Today she has learned to accept the colour and even have fun with it. It also represents hope that Indigenous families and communities are healing, and it has become a symbol of defiance and commitment to a better future. By wearing an orange shirt on Orange Shirt Day, you are making a statement that Residential Schools were wrong and that you commit to the concept that
EVERY CHILD MATTERS.

Artwork by grade 7 student Abby Billard from Harold Peterson Middle School.

THIS IS PHYLLIS'S MESSAGE TO YOU

 Phyllis (Jack) Webstad

Dear Reader,

It seems like from the very beginning that this whole "Orange Shirt Movement" has been divinely guided. For whatever reason, I was chosen to do this work, whether I was ready or not. Things just happened without a lot of trying on my part. People, places and events just fell into place. I've often wondered why me? As soon as I'd think why me, I would tell myself - Why not me? When I was putting together my presentation for speaking and wondering about why my story is so accepted, I thought about it and came up with this: Why is my story so accepted?

- Children – easy to understand.
- Non-Indigenous People – can associate.
- Residential School Survivors and their families –also their story.
- It opens the door to discussion, in a gentle way, about a heavy topic.
- It is time.

My story is easy for children to understand. They can associate with shopping for going back to school, how exciting that is. They can then empathize with how it would feel to have someone take something away that their parents bought for their first day of school.

Non-Indigenous people have children, grandchildren, nieces, nephews. They can empathize and think of what it would feel like to have their children suddenly snatched from their homes and arms and be absolutely helpless to do anything about it. They cannot imagine!

My story is not unique, Residential School Survivors and their families can associate with my orange shirt story. Residential Schools happened in Canada from top to bottom, left to right. There are many stories (truths) that need to be and are being told. Families of Survivors are finding out why their lives are the way they are after understanding what their parents or grand-parents had to live through and how that experience is impacting their lives.

The topic of Residential Schools isn't pleasant. I offer my story in a gentle way as a conversation starter, a door opener to discussion about all aspects of Indian Residential School.

And lastly, it is time. It is time our truths be heard. It's time that non-Indigenous Canadians know the history of Indian Residential Schools. The Truth and Reconciliation Commission went across Canada and was wrapping up its tour in 2013 when they came to Williams Lake, B.C. Canadians were ready to keep the conversation happening after the TRC wrapped up.

I pledge to continue to do my best to be the face of the Orange Shirt movement. I've already met so many amazing people on my travels across Canada and I've come to witness and realize that our future is in good hands. The children in elementary and high schools get it, they are the generation that will change our society for the better and make sure that this never happens again.

I thank everyone that participates and wears an orange shirt on Orange Shirt Day which is also the National Day for Truth and Reconciliation. By wearing an orange shirt, that means you care about what happened to us and that you are taking the time to learn. To us Survivors, it is a little bit of justice in our lifetime for what happened to us. We won't be around forever, one day there will be no Survivors left in Canada. My hope is Orange Shirt Day will continue to be the vehicle in telling the history long after we are gone.

Thank you for taking the time to learn about my story and about Orange Shirt Day. Please know that I do spend countless hours online looking at pictures, watching videos and reading about what you all are doing. I've always been a person who needs to know everything, it's taken me a while to comprehend that I will never know everything that is happening for Orange Shirt Day. So Kukstemcw, thank you, keep doing what you're doing.

I want to finish my message to you by saying that I do not claim to represent or speak for other Survivors or their families. I share my story and my family's story, which does not represent all other people's thoughts, experiences or perspectives.

All My Relations.

Phyllis W.

ORANGE SHIRT SOCIETY

The Orange Shirt Society is a non-profit organization, based in Williams Lake, B.C., which grew out of the events in 2013, inspired by Chief Fred Robbins' vision for reconciliation. The Orange Shirt Society board is composed of diverse members dedicated to raising awareness of the Residential Schools and supporting the development of Orange Shirt Day.

The Society's purposes: [16]

1.) To support Indian Residential School Reconciliation

2.) To create awareness of the individual, family and community intergenerational impacts of Indian Residential Schools though Orange Shirt Society activities

3.) To create awareness of the concept of "Every Child Matters"

Phyllis Webstad and the Orange Shirt Society would like to take this opportunity to thank you for supporting our journey towards Truth and Reconciliation and honouring our Residential School Survivors. This year (2023) will mark 10 years since Phyllis shared her story publicly for the first time, which lead to the creation of the first Orange Shirt Day in 2013.

We are encouraged that you have purchased this book and are taking the opportunity to reflect on Phyllis' truths that she shares within its pages. Thank you for increasing your awareness and helping us aim towards having these books placed in every classroom across Canada.

Having our books in classrooms all over Canada will help to achieve our journey in Truth and Reconciliation and honour all Indian Residential School Survivors as well as intergenerational survivors. This book is intended to provide you with knowledge that may not have been taught in previous history lessons you've experienced and will help guide and support the future conversations you may have. Canadians have the opportunity to honour all of the calls to action of the Truth and Reconciliation Commission and this book helps to address Call to Action #6 - Education.

Each year for the Orange Shirt Society, September 30th begins with the support of events across the country named Orange Shirt Day. From there, the momentum is driven throughout the rest of the year with programs and presentations in schools, communities, organizations, and businesses to engage people in relearning history and acting on Truth and Reconciliation in their spheres of influence. Some of our programs include but not exclusively the Orange Jersey Project, the Healing Garden Project, Storyteller Project, and Every Child Matters Crosswalk Program.

As we step into our 10th anniversary, we want to enhance our commitment to engaging more people with programs that will help with Healing. Please join on us on September 30th to honour, respect and uplift our survivors.

Shannon Henderson
President of Orange Shirt Society

CHAPTER ONE QUESTIONS

REFLECTION ON LEARNING

1. What is the way to achieve Indian Residential School reconciliation according to the book? How is this happening? Whose responsibility is it? What is your role in this process?
2. Why is it better to refer to Canada's First Peoples as Indigenous or Aboriginal instead of "Indian"? What effect might shifting to calling them Indigenous from "Indian" have on how they are perceived?
3. What was Chief Fred Robbins' vision? Who did it include?
4. What was the purpose of the Truth and Reconciliation Commission founded on June 2, 2008?
5. What was the goal of the Truth and Reconciliation Commission?
6. Why did Stephen Harper apologize on June 11th, 2008?
7. Where did Canada's apology to Indigenous people for Residential Schools take place? Why did they choose to do it there?
8. Why was this apology significant to the process of Truth and Reconciliation?
9. Who is Phyllis Webstad? What connection does she have to Orange Shirt Day?
10. Provide 3 facts about Phyllis Webstad that relate to her Residential School experience.
11. Where did Phyllis Webstad get her orange shirt from? Was the shirt ever returned to her?
12. What message does she spread? Why did she want to share her own story?
13. What is the significance of orange being the chosen colour of shirt for this commemorative Day?
14. What are the purposes of the Orange Shirt Society? How do they support Truth and Reconciliation?
15. What is the central message of the Orange Shirt Society? Why is it a message for all Canadians?
16. The Truth and Reconciliation Commission of Canada (TRC) provided 94 Calls to Action to implement change in Canada. Why do you think the TRC used words such as "Calls to Action" versus suggestions? Reflect on the difference between these words and their impacts.
17. In Phyllis Webstad's letter to you, the reader, she says "by wearing an orange shirt, what that means is that you care about what happened to us and that you are taking the time to learn. To us Survivors, it is a little bit of justice in our lifetime for what happened to us." Why do you think Phyllis says "a little bit of justice" instead of "complete justice"? Do you think it is possible to have complete justice for what happened to Indigenous people?
18. Why do you think the Orange Shirt Society and Phyllis Webstad teach us the phrase "Every Child Matters"? Why do you think the Orange Shirt Society uses the phrase "Every Child Matters" and who are they referring to?

RESEARCH

Stephen Harper apologized in 2008 for the Canadian Government's role in Residential Schools. Find the transcript of the apology. Why do you think the Canadian Government chose this time in history to issue an official apology for Residential Schools? What was the response of Indigenous peoples? To what extent do you think this has changed things for Indigenous peoples in Canada? What might be the next steps in the process of true reconciliation?

ACTIVITY

Phyllis Webstad wrote you a letter to encourage and thank you for taking the time to read this book, learn about Orange Shirt Day and participate in reconciliation. Now it's your turn. Write a letter to Phyllis Webstad. You may consider asking Phyllis questions or sharing your thoughts.

> As someone whos never faced discrimination based on my skin tone and history, its hard to fully understand how this must feel for Indigenous people. I've never had to go through this sort of suffering before but people of my colour have inflicted this pain on people countless times. It's important to me that we end the cycle of suffering for these people though I think many of these people will never get to feel free of those feelings and it upsets me that I can't do anything about that. But, growing up as someone whos part of the LGBT community, I understand why they would not be able to forgive and move on and I'm not bothered by them feeling this way as we cannot fix all the suffering that has happened or will continue to happen. We can only truely teach love and acceptance to ourselves for the future.

SOURCES

1. 18"National Day for Truth and Reconciliation". Government of Canada. November 15th, 2022. <https://www.canada.ca/en/canadian-heritage/campaigns/national-day-truth-reconciliation.html> Accessed November 22nd, 2022.
2. "Indian." The Canadian Encyclopedia. May 11, 2020. <https://thecanadianencyclopedia.ca/en/article/indian-term> accessed May 15, 2020.
3. "Archived - Common Terminology." Indigenous and Northern Affairs Canada. March 11, 2013. <https://www.aadnc-aandc.gc.ca/eng/1358879361384/1358879407462> accessed May 1, 2020.
4. "Terminology." Indigenous Foundations UBC Arts. <https://indigenousfoundations.arts.ubc.ca/terminology/#rstnations> accessed May 1, 2020.
5. "Archived - Common Terminology." Indigenous and Northern Affairs Canada. March 11, 2013. <https://www.aadnc-aandc.gc.ca/eng/1358879361384/1358879407462> accessed May 1, 2020.
6. "Citizenship." Métis National Council. Source quotes R. v. Powley 2003, the Supreme Court of Canada. <https://www.metisnation.ca/about/citizenship>.Accessed November 16, 2022.
7. Williams Lake Band. <https://williamslakeband.ca/> accessed April 30, 2020.
8. "Truth and Reconciliation Commission: By the numbers." CBC News. Daniel Schwartz. June 3, 2015. <https://www.cbc.ca/news/indigenous/truth-and-reconciliation-commission-by-the-numbers-1.3096185> accessed May 1, 2020.
   "Residential Schools Findings Point to 'Cultural Genocide,' commission chair says." CBC News. John Paul Tasker. May 15, 2015. <https://www.cbc.ca/news/politics/residential-schools-ndings-point-to-cultural-genocide-commission-chair-says-1.3093580> accessed March 30, 2020.
   "'This is heavy truth': Tk'emlúps te Secwépemc chief says more to be done to identify unmarked graves". CBC. <https://www.cbc.ca/news/canada/british-columbia/kamloops-residential-school-findings-1.6084185> accessed on November 30th, 2022.
9. Tarbell, Harold. St. Joseph's Mission Residential School Commemoration Project Document. Remembering, Recovering, and Reconciling. Williams Lake: Tarbell Facilitation Network, 2013.
10. "Chief Fred Robbins Speech." Boitanio Park Monument Unveiling. The Commemoration Project Events. Filmed by John Dell. Signal Point Media, 2013. DVD.
11. "A Timeline of Residential Schools, the Truth and Reconciliation Commission." CBC News. May 16, 2008. < https://www.cbc.ca/news/canada/a-timeline-of-residential-schools-the-truth-and-reconciliation-commission-1.724434> accessed December. 1, 2019.
12 "Government Apology to Former Students of Indian Residential Schools." The Canadian Encyclopedia. April 15, 2015. <https://thecanadianencyclopedia.ca/en/article/government-apology-to-former-students-of-indian-residential-schools> accessed April 30, 2020.
    "Residential School." Truth and Reconciliation Commission. <http://www.trc.ca/about-us.html> accessed October 15, 2019.
13. "Truth and Reconciliation Commission of Canad": Calls to Action." Truth and Reconciliation Commission of Canada. 2015. <http://trc.ca/assets/pdf/Calls_to_Action_English2.pdf> accessed February 1, 2020.
14. Tarbell, Harold. St. Joseph's Mission Residential School Commemoration Project Document. Remembering, Recovering, and Reconciling. Williams Lake: Tarbell Facilitation Network, 2013.
15. Tarbell, Harold. St. Joseph's Mission Residential School Commemoration Project Document. Remembering, Recovering, and Reconciling. Williams Lake: Tarbell Facilitation Network, 2013.
16. "Orange Shirt Society." Orange Shirt Day. <https://www.orangeshirtday.org/orange-shirt-society.html> accessed May 1, 2020.

A view of Saint Joseph's Mission Residential School in Williams Lake, BC. This is the Residential School that Phyllis Webstad attended. Photo by Dave Abott.

2 SETTING THE STAGE
TO RESIDENTIAL SCHOOLS

In order to understand the importance of Orange Shirt Day, we must go back to the beginning and learn about the events that led to the creation of **Indian Residential Schools** in Canada. By understanding the mistakes made by past governments, and others throughout history, they can be prevented from happening in the future.

Orange Shirt Day is about ensuring that everyone understands the impacts of the Residential School System. Everyone must recognize that the Residential School System and events that occurred within the system were wrong, and that they feel empowered to help prevent these mistakes from ever happening again.

Before one can start talking about Residential Schools and their impacts, there are a few things you need to be aware of. Let's start at the very beginning, before Europeans and Indigenous people came into contact.

Indian Residential Schools (also referred to as Industrial schools)
"Residential Schools for Aboriginal people in Canada date back to the 1870s. Over 130 Residential Schools were located across the country, and the last school closed in 1996. These government-funded, church-run schools were set up to eliminate parental involvement in the intellectual, cultural, and spiritual development of Aboriginal children. During this era, more than 150,000 First Nations, Métis, and Inuit children were placed in these schools often against their parents' wishes. Many were forbidden to speak their language and practice their own culture. While there is an estimated 80,000 former students living today, the ongoing impact of Residential Schools has been felt throughout generations and has contributed to social problems that continue to exist."[1] The TRC only referred to Canadian government run schools. There were other Residential Schools and Day Schools across the country as early as 1620, run by churches and other organizations.[2]

INDIGENOUS SOCIETY BEFORE CONTACT

For a long time, Indigenous people lived in what is now known as North America before Europeans arrived. All of these Indigenous cultures were unique yet they shared common worldviews. Indigenous communities had their own oral histories, common laws and ways of being.

*"**Historically Aboriginal people throughout North America lived in successful and dynamic societies. These societies have their own languages, history, cultures, spirituality, technologies, and values.** The security and survival of these societies depended on passing on this legacy from one generation to the next. Aboriginal peoples did this through a seamless mixture of teachings, ceremonies, and daily activities. While differing in specifics from one people to another, traditional Aboriginal teachings described a coherent, interconnected world."* [3]

Alicia Mae Cardinal performs a women's fancy orange shawl & dress dance special at a 2019 Pow Wow in Kamloops, B.C. Photo is by Peter Olsen of Olsen Imaging.

COLONIZATION IN CANADA

As Europeans began to explore and **colonize** this side of the world, Indigenous communities became threatened.[4] The government and the new settlers wanted to develop Indigenous land, but the Indigenous communities rightfully did not want to leave their traditional territories. As a result, the government and new settlers began mistreating the Indigenous people in a variety of cruel ways.

As European immigrants settled in Canada, they brought several diseases that gravely impacted the Indigenous people who did not have a natural immunity.[5] In 1862, a smallpox outbreak began in Victoria B.C., and then it spread to Indigenous communities throughout B.C. The outbreak of smallpox resulted in the deaths of approximately half of B.C.'s Indigenous population leaving their land vulnerable for colonization.[6] The authorities in Victoria, B.C., could have prevented the smallpox epidemic yet chose not to, resulting in the deaths of thousands of Indigenous people in British Columbia, which has been considered an act of genocide.[7]

Several years later, the Indian Act was created to continue the efforts to remove Indigenous people, their cultures and their traditions from Canada.

Artwork by grade 12 student Lauren Nichols.

Colonize occurs when settlers attempt to take over foreign land by forcefully imposing their own politics and culture.

THE INDIAN ACT

In 1876, the Canadian Government passed a law called the **Indian Act**. The purpose of the Indian Act was to control, marginalize and oppress Indigenous people.[8]

The Indian Act gave the government political power enabling them to control the Indigenous population by regulating their languages, traditions, customs and lands. Indigenous people were required to register themselves and even live on government allotted land.

The Indian Act was maintained by the Department of Indian Affairs and Northern Development. Indian Agents were employed to ensure the Indigenous people were obeying the law; Indigenous people were completely stripped of their freedoms. The Indian Act is still in force today.

*"...the Indian Act... brought together all of Canada's legislation governing Indian people. The act both defined who Indians were under Canadian law and set out the process by which people would cease to be Indians. **Under the act, the Canadian Government assumed control of Indian peoples' governments, economy, religion, land, education, and even their personal lives.** The act empowered the federal cabinet to depose Chiefs and overturn* **band** *decisions—and the government used this authority to control band governments... Provisions in the Indian Act prohibited Indians from participating in sacred ceremonies such as the Potlatch on the West Coast and the Sun Dance on the Prairies. Indians could not own reserve land as individuals... **The act placed new restrictions on Aboriginal hunting rights. The government had the power to move the bands if reserve land was needed by growing towns and cities.**"* [9]

Indian Act is a Canadian federal law enacted in 1876 that allowed the government the regimented management of Indigenous people and reserve lands. The purpose of the Indian Act was to control, marginalize and oppress Indigenous people. [10]

A Band "or 'Indian Band', is a governing unit of Indians in Canada instituted by the Indian Act, 1876. The Indian Act defines a 'band' as a 'body of Indians.'" [11]

LAND TAKEN

After the Indian Act was created, it shifted the life of Indigenous people in many negative ways including the loss of ability to practice cultural ceremonies, the loss of hunting rights and the implementation of government control over Indigenous communities.[12] The government wanted land and resources. Indigenous people were deemed to be in the way. Their land was taken and reserves were established often on useless infertile land, confining most Indigenous people to a specific area. [13]

INDIAN AGENTS

The **Indian Agent** was an administrator or representative for the Canadian government who had authority over Indigenous people and reserve lands.[14] As Phyllis Webstad explained "The Indian Agent had more power than the Chiefs and the Matriarchs." [15]

Artwork by Brock Nicol from Phyllis Webstad's children's book, *The Orange Shirt Story*.

ROYAL CANADIAN MOUNTED POLICE

The Royal Canadian Mounted Police played a role in the Indian Residential School System by responding to various law-enforcement related requests from Indian Agents and the Department of Indian Affairs. These requests included retrieving children who had run away from Residential School and fining families for not sending their children to Residential School. [16]

THE CREATION OF THE RESIDENTIAL SCHOOLS SYSTEM

When Indigenous children lived within their communities, prior to the creation of the Residential School System, Indigenous families had the ability to continue passing on cultural identity and customs to their children. In 1879, John A. MacDonald declared "it has been strongly impressed upon myself, as head of the [Indian] department, that Indian children should be withdrawn as much as possible from the parental influence, and the only way to do that would be to put them in central training industrial schools where they will acquire the habits and modes of thought of white men." [17]

John A Macdonald wanted to remove the children from their families to assimilate them into European-like culture. "[He] moved a measure through his cabinet authorizing the creation of three Residential Schools for Aboriginal children... What existed prior to 1883 was not a Residential School system, but a series of individual church-led initiatives... The federal government decision in that year to open three new schools on the prairies marked... the beginning of Canada's Residential School System." [18]

The first Residential School in Canada was called the Mohawk Institute; it is pictured here in 1943. The original school building was destroyed by fire in the 1850s and the replacement building was also destroyed by fire in 1903. The building pictured here served as the Mohawk Institute from 1904 to 1970 when it closed. Photo courtesy of the Shingwauk Residential Schools Centre of Algoma University.

John A Macdonald "As both prime minister and minister of Indian Affairs, Macdonald was responsible for Indigenous policy, including the development of the Residential School system and increasingly repressive measures against Indigenous populations." [19]

In 1920, the Canadian Government changed the Indian Act *"to require school-aged Indian children to attend school."* [20] Indigenous children were now required to attend Residential School whether they wanted to or not. Initially there were three government sponsored Residential Schools in 1883. By 1931 there were eighty government sponsored Residential Schools across Canada. Duncan Campbell Scott, who succeeded John A Macdonald as Minister of Indian Affairs, announced, *"I want to get rid of the Indian problem… Our objective is to continue until there is not an Indian that has not been absorbed into the body politic, and there is no Indian question, and no Indian Department..."* [21]

Residential Schools were used as a way to remove Indigenous people, their cultures and their traditions from within Canada. The early to mid 1900s saw a dramatic rise in the quantity of Residential Schools, thus more and more children were separated from their families and communities.

*...those of you who are interested in the Residential School story need to understand something that is very important, that it isn't just about Residential Schools. **They [the Canadian Government] took our children away from us and placed them in the schools so that they could indoctrinate them into a different way of thinking...** then they proceeded to go out and try to destroy the villages. So they undermined our leadership, they took away the power of Chiefs, they took away the power of women, they took away the power of our culture, they prohibited ceremonies, they prohibited gatherings, they prohibited all of the things that societies need to hold itself together. **As many Survivors have observed, they took away our power. They took away our power to be who we were meant to be.***

- Truth And Reconciliation Commission Chair Senator Murray Sinclair [22]

Senator Murray Sinclair speaking on reconciliation at King's University on September 26, 2019. Photo taken by Michael Swan of the Catholic Register.

The Canadian Government was intentional and systematic with their approach to settle the land and remove any trace of Indigenous peoples and their cultural practices.[23] Truth and Reconciliation Commission Chair Murray Sinclair described this as cultural **genocide** when delivering the report of the Commission.[24]

Understanding and learning the history of what happened before, during and after Residential Schools is critical to achieving reconciliation. Without knowing what happened and how it happened, change would be impossible. Through educating yourself on the creation of the Indian Act, the horrible things that followed and the establishment of government-sponsored Residential Schools, you can begin the journey to become an agent of true change.

A view outside St. Joseph's Mission Residential School (also known as Williams Lake Indian School). Year unknown. Photo courtesy of Fonds Deschâtelets, Archives Deschâtelets-NDC.

Genocide "means any of the following acts committed with intent to destroy, in whole or in part, a national, ethnical, racial or religious group, as such: Killing members of the group; Causing serious bodily or mental harm to members of the group; Deliberately inflicting on the group conditions of life calculated to bring about its physical destruction in whole or in part; Imposing measures intended to prevent births within the group; Forcibly transferring children of the group to another group." [25]

CHAPTER TWO QUESTIONS

REFLECTION ON LEARNING

1. Before European contact with Indigenous peoples, what was life like for the Indigenous peoples living on the land now known as North America?

2. Based on the text, what impacts did European settlers have on Indigenous communities? Provide some examples of these effects and why there might be a need to address these before reconciliation can occur.

3. Why did the European immigrants not suffer as much from the diseases they brought to Canada compared to the Indigenous people?

4. Why would authorities choosing not to prevent the spread of the smallpox disease that resulted in the death of thousands of Indigenous people in B.C. be considered an act of genocide? What is your perspective about this?

5. What purpose did the Indian Act that was passed in 1876 have? What types of things did the Indian Act control for Indigenous peoples?

6. The attitudes of John A. Macdonald and other people have had a lasting impact on laws enacted in the Indian Act. To what extent and in what ways has this affected Indigenous peoples living in Canada?

7. What is the reserve system in Canada? What was its purpose? How did it divide Indigenous peoples?

8. What roles did Indian Agents and the RCMP play in the Residential School System and ensuring other laws included in the Indian Act were followed? How might that affect their relationships with Indigenous peoples in Canada today?

9. In 1883, John A MacDonald made a decision that drastically impacted Indigenous children and their families. What was that decision?

10. What change did the Canadian Government make to the Indian Act in 1920? What was the purpose for this change? What effect did this have on Indigenous children and families?

11. What did Duncan Campbell Scott say about the "Indian problem"? What do you think about this statement and what effect might it have had?

12. What does Senator Murray Sinclair state about Residential Schools? What do you think about this statement and why do you think this?

13. By 1931, how many government-sponsored Residential Schools existed in Canada? Why do you think it is important to know the number?

14. Based on what you have learned so far, do you think that genocide took place in Canada? If so, to what extent does this affect Canadians today, and why are all Canadians encouraged to walk a path of Truth and Reconciliation?

15. The Indian Act was designed to control, marginalize, and oppress Indigenous people. What do you think the people who created the Indian Act thought about Indigenous people at the time? Explain fully.

16. In 1920, Indigenous children were forced into the Residential School System by the Canadian government making it mandatory for children to attend Residential Schools. In what ways and to what extent do you think this impacted Indigenous children, families, and their communities?

17. The Orange Shirt Society believes reconciliation requires each of us to have a thorough understanding of Canadian and Indigenous history before, during, and after the Indian Residential School System. Why do you think it is important to understand and talk about this history in order to truly achieve reconciliation?

18. Sir John A. Macdonald stated in the House of Commons in 1885 that "we have been pampering and coaxing the Indians; that we must take a new course, we must vindicate the position of the white man, we must teach the Indians what law is; we must not pauperise them, as they say we have been doing."[26] Discuss your response to Macdonald's statement in relation to what you have learned. To what extent do you believe this is still affecting the relationship between Indigenous peoples and other Canadians today.

RESEARCH

1. Look up the Indian Act. How does the Indian Act continue to affect Indigenous peoples in Canada today? What stands out most for you in the current Indian Act? Explain fully your understanding of the effects this may still have on Indigenous peoples in Canada.

2. What are the traditional systems of governance in Indigenous communities? How do they operate? What is the role of a Chief or Matriarch in some communities? Please note, there is a variety and diversity of cultures and, therefore, the same can be found in traditional governing systems. In your research, ensure you honour specific cultures and peoples.

TIMELINE ACTIVITY

Complete the following timeline activity. Use the book and your own research if needed to create a timeline with the events of what took place.

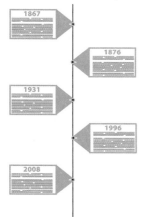

Dates:
1867, 2008, 1883, 1600s, 1876, 1996, 1931, 1920

Events:
First Non-Government-Sponsored Residential Schools Established

Date Canada Became a Country

Indian Act Becomes Law

Residential School System Becomes Government-Sponsored

Changes to Indian Act Making it Mandatory for Indigenous Children to Attend Residential Schools

By This Time There Were 80 Government-Sponsored Residential Schools

Last Government-Sponsored Residential School was Closed

The Canadian Government Issued an Apology to Indigenous People for their Role in Residential Schools

SOURCES

1. "Residential School." Truth and Reconciliation Commission. <http://www.trc.ca/about-us.html> accessed October 15, 2020.
2. The Truth and Reconciliation Commission of Canada. They Came for the Children. Manitoba: Library and Archives Canada Cataloguing in Publication, 2012. pp. 5.
3. The Truth and Reconciliation Commission of Canada. They Came for the Children. Manitoba: Library and Archives Canada Cataloguing in Publication, 2012. pp. 7.
4. "Indigenous History in Canada." Indigenous and Northern Affairs Canada. August 14, 2018. <https://www.aadnc-aandc.gc.ca/eng/1100100013778/1100100013779> accessed February 1, 2020.
5. "The Impacts of Smallpox on First Nations on the West Coast." Indigenous Corporate Training. April 17, 2017. <https://www.ictinc.ca/blog/the-impact-of-small-pox-on-rst-nations-on-the-west-coast> accessed May 1, 2020.
6. "Smallpox in Canada." The Canadian Encyclopedia. February 12, 2020. <https://www.thecanadianencyclopedia.ca/en/article/smallpox> accessed May 28, 2020.
7. "How a smallpox epidemic forged modern British Columbia." Maclean's. August 1st, 2017. <https://www.macleans.ca/news/canada/how-a-smallpox-epidemic-forged-modern-british-columbia/> accessed on November 22nd, 2022.
8. The Truth and Reconciliation Commission of Canada. They Came for the Children. Manitoba: Library and Archives Canada Cataloguing in Publication, 2012. pp. 18.
9. The Truth and Reconciliation Commission of Canada. They Came for the Children. Manitoba: Library and Archives Canada Cataloguing in Publication, 2012. pp. 11.
10. The Truth and Reconciliation Commission of Canada. They Came for the Children. Manitoba: Library and Archives Canada Cataloguing in Publication, 2012. pp. 11.
11. "Bands." Indigenous Foundations UBC Arts. <https://indigenousfoundations.arts.ubc.ca/bands/>, accessed May 25, 2020.
12. "Reserves." The Canadian Encyclopedia, July 12, 2018. < https://www.thecanadianencyclopedia.ca/en/article/aboriginal-reserves> accessed May 28, 2020.
13. "Canada's Residential Schools: The History, Part 1 Origins to 1939." Truth and Reconciliation Commission of Canada. 2015. <http://www.trc.ca/assets/pdf/Volume_1_History_Part_1_English_Web.pdf> accessed May 30, 2020. pp. 3.
14. "Indian Agents in Canada." The Canadian Encyclopedia, October 25, 2018. < https://www.thecanadianencyclopedia.ca/en/article/indian-agents-in-canada> accessed May 28, 2020.
15. Webstad, Phyllis. Personal Interview. January. 2020.
16. "The Role of the Royal Canadian Mounted Police During the Indian Residential School System. "Government of Canada. Marcel-Eugéne LeBeuf. April 3, 2013. <http://publications.gc.ca/site/eng/9.651577/publication.html> accessed April 30, 2020.
17. "10 Quotes John A. Macdonald Made About First Nations." Indigenous Corporate Training. June 28, 2016. < https://www.ictinc.ca/blog/10-quotes-john-a.-macdonald-made-about-rst-nations> accessed May 28, 2020.
18. The Truth and Reconciliation Commission of Canada. They Came for the Children. Manitoba: Library and Archives Canada Cataloguing in Publication, 2012. pp. 5-6.
19. "Sir John A Macdonald." The Canadian Encyclopedia. <https://www.thecanadianencyclopedia.ca/en/article/sir-john-alexander-macdonald> accessed on November 30th, 2022
20. The Truth and Reconciliation Commission of Canada. They Came for the Children. Manitoba: Library and Archives Canada Cataloguing in Publication, 2012. pp. 12.
"Indian Residential Schools and Reconciliation: 1920-1927 Indian Act Becomes More Restrictive." First Nations Education Steering Committee. <http://www.fnesc.ca/wp/wp-content/uploads/2015/07/IRSR11-12-DE-1920-1927.pdf> accessed May 28, 2020.
21. "10 Quotes John A. Macdonald Made About First Nations." Indigenous Corporate Training. June 28, 2016. < https://www.ictinc.ca/blog/10-quotes-john-a.-macdonald-made-about-rst-nations> accessed May 28, 2020.
22. "Justice and Federal Commissioner Murray Sinclair Speech." Truth and Reconciliation Commission. The Commemoration Project Events. Filmed by John Dell. Signal Point Media, 2013. DVD.
23. "Canada's Residential Schools: The History, Part 1 Origins to 1939." Truth and Reconciliation Commission of Canada. 2015. <http://www.trc.ca/assets/pdf/Volume_1_History_Part_1_English_Web.pdf> accessed May 30, 2020. pp. 4.
24. "Residential Schools Finding Point to 'Cultural Genocide,' Commission Chair Say." CBC News. John Paul Tasker. May 30, 2015. <https://www.cbc.ca/news/politics/residential-schools-ndings-point-to-cultural-genocide-commission-chair-says-1.3093580> accessed January 15, 2020.
25. "Genocide." United Nations Oce on Genocide Prevention and the Responsibility to Protect. <https://www.un.org/en/genocideprevention/genocide.shtml> accessed February 15, 2020.
26. "10 Quotes John A. Macdonald Made About First Nations." Indigenous Corporate Training. June 28, 2016. <https://www.ictinc.ca/blog/10-quotes-john-a.-macdonald-made-about-rst-nations> accessed May 28, 2020.

Orange Shirt Day inspired artwork by grade 11 student Mikayla Schreiner.

3 RESIDENTIAL SCHOOLS
THEIR IMPACTS ON INDIGENOUS PEOPLE

In order for us to begin the process of truth and reconciliation, it is crucial to understand the truth about what happened to Indigenous people at Residential Schools, the ongoing impacts, and our personal responsibility to work towards reconciliation.

It is estimated that approximately 150,000 Indigenous children attended government- sponsored Canadian Residential Schools.[1] At least 6000 of those children died at Residential Schools due to a variety of reasons including abuse, overcrowding, malnourishment, neglect, poor health and trying to run away.[2] In Canada and the United States, there are processes underway to raise awareness about, honour, and in some cases reclaim children that are being discovered buried in unmarked graves at Residential School sites.[3] These government Residential Schools ran between 1883 and 1996. As of 2015, it was estimated that there were over 80,000 Survivors of Residential Schools. [4]

Chief Fred Robbins' vision of reconciling requires all people to understand the truths of what happened in Residential Schools and for this history to be taught in schools. When everyone understands and acknowledges the truths of the impact of Residential Schools, reconciling our differences and finding a path forward for a better future becomes possible.

It is important to remember each Residential School Survivor may have had a different experience but there are common stories amongst all Survivors.

THE LOCATION OF RESIDENTIAL SCHOOLS

Many Residential Schools were in isolated locations across Canada. This was a deliberate strategy of the government to remove children from their parental and cultural influences.

*"When the school is on the reserve, **the child lives with his parents who are savages; he is surrounded by savages,** and though he may learn to read and write, his habits and training and mode of thought are Indian."*

-John A Macdonald [5]

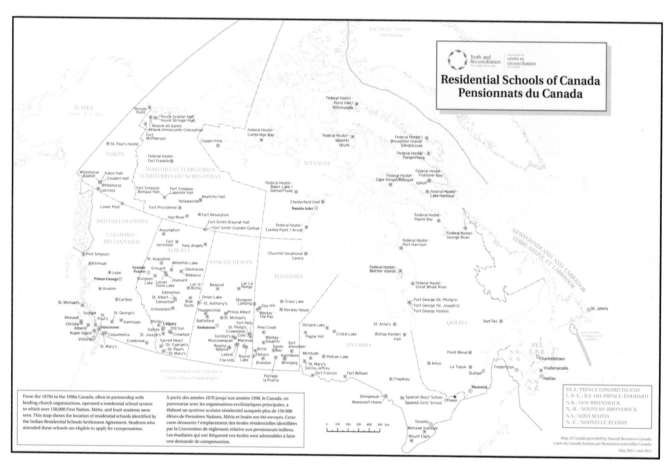

Truth and Reconciliation Commission map showing only government funded Residential Schools in Canada.

In 1920, the Indian Act was amended to require all Indigenous children to attend Residential School.[6] Indigenous families had no choice, and the Canadian government forced children to leave their parents and families behind to attend Residential School when they were as young as four years old. Children were isolated and deprived of their families, culture, language, communities and security.

Phyllis Webstad and her aunt, Agness Jack, at the first Orange Shirt Day event in Williams Lake in 2013. Photo taken by Monica Lamb-Yorski of the Williams Lake Tribune.

I was six years old, and I'll never forget seeing that place for the first time. We came through the Onward Ranch and I got this terrible feeling - you know, like you have to not feel emotions any more? *Like they're pushed down - and I just knew I was going to prison.*

- Residential School Survivor Agness Jack, Aunt of Phyllis Webstad [7]

Young boy named Thomas Moore is pictured before and after he was admitted to the Regina Indian Industrial School in May of 1874. This photo is courtesy of Library and Archives Canada and the Annual Report of the Department of Indian Affairs, 1896/OCLC 1771148.

THE ARRIVAL AT RESIDENTIAL SCHOOLS

The arrival at Residential School was traumatic and difficult for many children.

"The assault on Aboriginal Identity began the moment the child took the first step across the school's threshold… Braided hair, which often has spiritual significance, was cut." [8]

When children arrived at Residential School their hair was cut and they were stripped of their clothes. Residential School Survivors have noted harsh chemicals were used to clean children upon arrival. In some cases, children were given a number and referred to by that number instead of their name. Some Survivors reported being given a new name entirely.

Cutting children's hair and taking away their names and clothes were the first steps in stripping children of their identity and self-worth.

LIFE AT RESIDENTIAL SCHOOLS

Life at the Residential Schools was traumatic and regimented. Days were filled with chores and religious teachings. Many children experienced unimaginable emotional, physical and sexual abuse creating trauma for which they were never given the opportunity or resources to heal. The Residential School housed children for the majority of the year and offered minimal, if any, education.[9] At Residential Schools, students were required to learn skills such as housekeeping and trades. Ultimately, their new skills served to keep the schools in operation as well as provided free labour for the school-run businesses. [10]

Students were swiftly and harshly punished for speaking their Indigenous languages. Due to funding issues, overcrowding and neglect "the schools could neither teach or care for children." [11]

A view inside St. Joseph's Mission Residential School (also know as Williams Lake Indian School) bedroom quarters with the students performing their prayers. Year unknown. Photo courtesy of Fonds Deschâtelets, Archives Deschâtelets-NDC.

A view inside the chapel at St. Joseph's Mission Residential School (also know as Williams Lake Indian School). Year unknown. Photo courtesy of Fonds Deschâtelets, Archives Deschâtelets-NDC.

RELIGIOUS INFLUENCE AT RESIDENTIAL SCHOOLS

Residential Schools in Canada were maintained and run by many religious groups including the Anglican, Baptist, Catholic, Mennonite, Non-denominational, Presbyterian and United Churches. The Canadian Government and churches not only wanted Indigenous people to adopt new western and colonial values, but they also wanted them to become more Christian. Residential Schools were staffed by members of these religious groups and churches who forced the students to suppress their own beliefs and adopt Christian values resulting in spiritual abuse. Their goal was to "civilize and Christianize" the students.[12] Many of these religious leaders took advantage of the students through emotional, physical and sexual abuses causing life long trauma that was later transmitted to other family members and generations.

> *"**Churches were eager to embrace the partnership [with government] because church missionary societies had laid the foundation for the system.** For most of the system's history, the churches had responsibility for the day-to-day operation of the schools... [the church] provided justification for undermining traditional spiritual leaders (who were treated as agents of the devil), **banning sacred cultural practices, and attempting to impose a new moral code on Aboriginal people by requiring them to abandon their traditional family structures.**"* [13]

ST. JOSEPH'S MISSION RESIDENTIAL SCHOOL

St. Joseph's Mission Residential School, or 'The Mission,' was the Residential School that both Phyllis Webstad and Chief Fred Robbins attended, among many other Survivors from the Cariboo region.

*"The St. Joseph's Mission Residential School... was founded and operated by the Oblates of Mary Immaculate, a French order of the Roman Catholic Church whose missionaries had been associated with the Cariboo region since the early days of contact and fur trading. **The St. Joseph's Mission was [originally one] of the earliest churches in the valley and is approximately 10km south of the City of Williams Lake. The school opened in 1872 and originally served as a day school for the children of miners.***

In 1891, the Oblate Fathers and the Federal Government agreed to operate the school exclusively as an industrial Residential School for native children... The 'official dates' for the operation of the school are July 19, 1891 to June 30,1981. The school buildings were eventually torn down and the property sold. Today, the foundation is all that remains of the school, along with the cemetery and the remainder of the property operates as a ranch." [14]

Rose Wilson Nee Jack, Phyllis's mother, attended St. Joseph's Mission Residential School and offers a glimpse into what her experience was:

"We must have been whispering loud. I admitted that it was me. The nun made me kneel in the large aisle. She forgot about me. In the wee hours of the morning, I finally got into my bed. There were rules, and when you broke them, you had to stand in the corner or kneel in the aisle. I remember being strapped but I don't remember what it was for, but it hurt because they used a ruler or a leather strap. I knew right from wrong and I tried my best to behave. I didn't like being strapped so I tried my best to obey the rules.
When I first started school, I used to wet my bed. It was humiliating. The supervisor would put my stinky, wet bed sheet on my head in front of the other children to see and taunt*... I never tried to run away because they just brought you back anyway, you can't get away, and I didn't want to be punished for it...*
The Residential School seemed like a prison sentence, it felt like I was never going to get out of there. *I was there for 10 years. I didn't understand why I was sent to Residential School at first, but then I learned they [my parents] would be sent to jail for not sending us there. They would take my mom or dad away because they wouldn't let them take us away to school."* [15]

St. Joseph's Mission Residential School was located just outside of Williams Lake, B.C. It opened in 1872 and closed in 1981. St. Joseph's Mission Residential School has also been called The Mission, Williams Lake Indian School, Williams Lake Industrial School, Cariboo Residential Industrial School and Cariboo Student Residence.

Historical photo of Saint Joseph's Mission Residential School. Photo courtesy of John Dell.

"

*The school was supported by an annual federal grant, but funding was a constant issue and often inadequate to support quality education, care of children, or facility maintenance. **The school was attended by children from the three nearby Nations, [the Secwépemc (Shuswap), the Tsilhqot'in (Chilcotin) and the Dakelh (Carrier)] as well as from the St'at'imc (Lillooet) Nation**...*

*Teaching methods at The Mission required unquestioning obedience, strict discipline and speaking only in English. Transgressions resulted in harsh punishment. Hunger was common, food often poor, and sickness rampant in the poorly constructed buildings. **The school attempted to destroy students' pride in their heritage, their families and themselves... The student death rate was high, and some who died were not returned to their parents.***

"

- Written by Ordell Steen, Jean William and Rick Gilbert in the *Orange Shirt Story*. [16]

Agness Jack photographed
by Darrin Andrews

Former St. Joseph's Mission Residential School student Agness Jack reflects on her horrific experience and the effects it had on her.

"

During that first year [at the Residential School], I contracted tuberculosis. I was sick for a long time, and they treated me very badly. I was very sick, and finally I was sent to Coqualeetza Indian Hospital in Sardis. It was a Residential School but they turned it into a sanitarium for Indian people with TB because there were so many of us. I was there four years, and it was a blessing in disguise because they treated us like people - you know, like you should get treated in a hospital when you are sick, and the food was way better. **It sure was a shock to me when I went back to the Mission - they called us by numbers instead of names, we were treated as kids without feelings.**

Once at Easter, after I got out, my mom wanted me to go to Mass on Easter Sunday. I told her that I went to church enough at the Mission to last me the rest of my life, and what good did it do me? That Bishop... preached the best sermons - he was the head of the school, the principal - and look what he did! He travelled with the girls in the pipe band, and he molested them - he drove the bus. He was tried in Vancouver but his case was dismissed or postponed on a technicality. I think the women just didn't have it in them to go through all that again. So he never paid for what he did.

I was working as a reporter for the Tribune when the place finally closed, and I went to cover the final Mass for the paper. I overheard the night watchman talking with another man, and he said, 'It's about time that place closed'. **Those children were supposed to be brought here for education, and instead they were sent to hell.** [17]

"

INTERGENERATIONAL TRAUMA

The trauma created by Residential Schools has created long-term impacts that have affected family members who did not attend a Residential School themselves. Many of the former students were unable to care for themselves or their families which created trauma passed down through the generations. Intergenerational trauma is still felt today within Indigenous communities.

*Many of us have not attended Residential School including myself but we feel the impacts, our children feel it, our grandchildren feel it. Today and yesterday is the beginning of a very small step in reconciliation between all communities and the Residential Schools that have impacted our First Nations people. I spoke yesterday about the high numbers of incarceration and low education levels of our First Nations People. The high number of children that are in care. Those are direct results and impacts from the Residential School. **We need to start someway to find a way to break that cycle and start having our people become healthier. It's an interesting and a long journey.***

- Former Chief Ann Louie of Williams Lake First Nations (T'exelcemc) [18]

Former Chief Ann Louie speaking at the May 17, 2013 unveiling of a commemorative monument in Boitanio Park, Williams Lake, BC. Film still courtesy of John Dell.

Life after Residential Schools has been extremely difficult and painful for many Indigenous people across Canada. The trauma and pain of Residential Schools has affected Survivors and their families creating intergenerational trauma.

Intergenerational trauma occurs when the trauma experienced by a parent or grandparent is also experienced by future generations, both emotionally and physically. The results of the intergenerational trauma caused by Residential Schools are catastrophic and have taken form in many ways such as alcoholism, abuse, mental illness and children being forced to live in foster care.[19]

As the government succeeded at suppressing traditional Indigenous skills and customs and separating children from their parents, the children were left parentless and unable to pass down traditional knowledge to their own families creating a significant loss of culture.

Intergenerational Survivors are Indigenous people who are still affected by the experiences of their ancestors who attended Residential Schools. The trauma has been transmitted from one family member to another due to the fact that the trauma runs so deep and that the Indigenous peoples were not provided with the resources to heal from their painful experiences.[20]

Nanenuŵes?in (I will see you again):
Karlene Harvey is a Tsilhqot'in and Syilx illustrator and writer, who lives on the unceded and ancestral home territories of the Musqueam, Squamish and Tseil-Waututh people. In her illustration on the right, Karlene depicts her late uncle Kelsey, who attended Residential School, carrying his childhood spirit on his shoulders.

> *"This image is in honour of my late Uncle Kelsey who passed away years after attending Residential School. My uncle is shown as an adult carrying his childhood spirit on his shoulders. As an adult, my uncle was a tough, loud guy and he wouldn't put up with mistreatment of himself, his loved ones and his nieces and nephews. **So much is unsaid about some of the complications and challenges he experienced in his lifetime due to Residential School but we knew he dealt with a lot. I see my uncle every time I meet a tough-as-nails youth.** A young person who has had to build up a thick exterior based on the accumulation of experiences and hardships they've faced and I honour these youth because they deserve our love, patience, and trust. My uncle deserved this, too."*[21]

Intergenerational survivor "refers to an individual who has been affected by the intergenerational dysfunction created by the experience of attending Residential School." [22]

Intergenerational trauma is the transmission of historical oppression and its negative consequences across generations. [23]

Orange Shirt Day Artwork by Karlene Harvey.

Another known impact of intergenerational trauma is lateral violence. Lateral violence happens when people who have experienced oppression suppress feelings such as anger, shame, and rage and can turn those feelings onto family or community members around them.

Phyllis Webstad shares her thoughts and experiences with oppression causing lateral violence, resulting in intergenerational trauma.

> *"An aunt told me a story about her grandmother. She would wake up her child by whipping them with a bridle and telling them to get up and look after her husband.* **When I asked my aunt why they were so mean to each other, she replied 'the Indian Act'.** *I was so confused, so my aunt explained to me that they were so oppressed, they had no option but to turn on each other. This family member was born in 1880, the Indian Act was enacted in 1876; she only knew being controlled by the Indian Agent.*
>
> *The account of this oppression reminded me of training I had taken regarding lateral violence. I still have that visual in my mind of when anything, for example, an orange, is pushed down upon, what happens? It quishes, it splats, it goes sideways.* **So when the Indian Act came into effect, the people were pushed down on, oppressed, and they couldn't fight back. They couldn't beat up the Indian Agent, they would go to jail. So what did they do? They laterally acted, they were mean to each other and beat on each other.**[24]*"*

For Phyllis, the biggest impact of intergenerational trauma was not growing up with a mother and a father. For Phyllis's son Jeremy, it is felt through the loss of culture and language because of the lasting effects of several generations of his family attending Residential School.

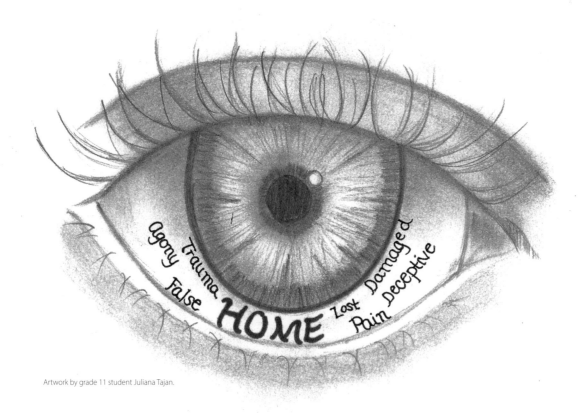

Artwork by grade 11 student Juliana Tajan.

"The Residential School System has impacted my grandmother — my mom's mom, my Granny Rose, my mom, they all went to school. [It's a] big impact because we lost our culture...
Language is the biggest barrier that I wish that we could get back, *we're never going to get it back. Language is gone in my opinion, all I have is a few words. I can't even teach my own children my language because we have no more teachers. The government did their job and took everything away from my family and all of the families that attended Residential School who lost their cultures, who lost their language....*
The past is something that cannot be erased but can be healed through education and knowledge. Learn through stories; you're never alone, don't be afraid, your voice is powerful. Learn to forgive and move forward."

- Jeremy Boston, Beyond the Orange Shirt Story [25]

Jeremy Boston photographed by Danielle Shack of DS Photography.

Orange Shirt Day acknowledges this intergenerational trauma and the pain experienced by Survivors and their families. Through this movement everyone is able to witness and share the collective truths of the trauma endured by not only Residential School Survivors, but their families thereafter.

In order to heal the wounds of the Residential School System, we must create a new legacy that "Every Child Matters." Through the acknowledgment of the painful truths of Residential Schools, and the cultural genocide that took place in Canada, we are able to begin healing and reconciling the trauma still felt today.

CHILDREN WHO DIDN'T COME HOME

In 2021,Tk'emlúps te Secwépemc First Nation announced the findings of 215 unmarked graves at the former Kamloops Indian Residential School. The Kamloops Indian Residential School was in operation from 1890 to 1978. The school was run by the Canadian federal government as well as the Catholic Church.[26]

IF WE HELD A MOMENT OF SILENCE 4 EACH CHILD WHO DIED IN RESIDENTIAL SCHOOL, WE'D BE SILENT FOR 13+ YRS

215 pairs of children's shoes displayed as part of a memorial at the Vancouver Art Gallery to honour the children found buried on the former Kamloops Indian Residential School site. Photo taken by Murray Lundberg on July 7, 2021.

Tk'emlúps te Secwépemc Kúkpi7 (Chief) Rosanne Casimir stated
"The truth is heavy...
We will follow the evidence as it is disclosed...
*We will follow the science while we pay heed to oral telling survivors share with us…. We are not here for retaliation, **we are here for truth telling, we are here today to honour the children.**"* [27]

In 2021, Stephanie Scott, executive director at the National Centre for Truth and Reconciliation, stated in an open letter:

*"The remains of 215 innocent children were found in unmarked graves on the former site of the Kamloops Indian Residential School. The horror, anger and grief shared collectively by Indigenous people across Turtle Island is as raw as it is heavy. **In our grief we hold ceremony, we bring little shoes to the steps of the perpetrators, we pour out our shared trauma on social media, we share contact information for crisis lines, we lower flags and turn the country orange.***
The mass gravesites of precious children whose lives were cut tragically short because of the Residential School system, like those recently uncovered on the traditional territory of the Tk'emlúps te Secwépemc people, have only been the subject of initial conversations with the Canadian government. This must change...

As Executive Director of the National Centre for Truth and Reconciliation (NCTR), the calls continue from media and they did not slow in what would typically be four days of mourning for some Indigenous People in Treaty One where the Centre is located. **There is a common theme of 'how could this happen?' in the questions raised. The answer is complex – rooted in racism and unjust policies, but as the former Manager of Statement Gathering during the Truth and Reconciliation Commission, I am not surprised this truth has finally come to light….**

For many, the Truth and Reconciliation Commission (TRC) was the first time Survivors and families could confront these questions in a safe space where there was common understanding. Sadly, it was the first time for many that they were believed and listened to…

This is just the beginning of recognizing the extent of horrific loss of precious lives caused by Residential Schools in Canada…

Since the close of the TRC, the NCTR has continued to build on the research and has confirmed the identities of 4,117 children who died… *The number of children in unmarked Residential School burial sites will increase as communities guide the search of the grounds of other sites. We owe it to these precious ones to remember, to grieve, and assert their memory as far more than a number, tweet or hashtag. While these commitments are largely considered positive, we need immediate action. We are losing our beloved Survivors daily and with them valuable insights that can help locate and identify the missing children. People for whom the actions of Residential Schools are not history, as coldly labeled by some, rather raw pain shared across families and generations scarred by the atrocities caused by church and nation.*

There are renewed calls for healing and supports to Indigenous communities and Indigenous leaders calling for radar ground searches at every Residential School site. **Let's honour these lost children by treating the Kamloops Residential School mass grave as a turning point to action. Survivors and their families deserve answers today.**" [28]

At St Joseph's Mission Residential School, where 3 generations of Phyllis Webstad's family attended, as of February 2023, after only searching 34 of the 782 hectares of land where the St. Joseph Mission Residential School was situated, they found 159 potential burial sites.

Truth comes before Reconciliation. Many Indigenous communities have begun the process of uncovering the truth of what took place at the Residential School sites across Canada and the United States. In some places, the names of children have been identified while other communities are still in process of determining the best course of action. [29]

Regardless of where Indigenous communities are at in the process, there is still a lot of work to be done, and part of that work is for all people to educate themselves of the truth.

With over 130 government sponsored Residential Schools that operated in Canada, the confirmations of missing children and unmarked burials will continue to increase in the coming months and years.

Charlene Belleau who attended St. Joseph's Mission Residential School for four years shares her truth about her grandfather, Allan Augustine. It was confirmed that he passed away at the Residential School. To date, it is unknown where his remains are buried.

"We have always known many of our children, our relatives, went to St.Joseph's Mission Indian Residential School and many never came home.

In 1920, my grandpa Augustine Allan committed suicide there, eating poisonous hemlock. Nine boys had a suicide pact, but only grandpa died, the others were saved. The priests or no one told our family about it, they buried him somewhere at St. Joseph's Mission IRS. **We don't know whether he even had a proper burial, suicide is not Catholic, and [we] have come to learn that they don't even have to report his death. To date, we have not been able to find a death certificate. The coroner of the day did not feel it was important to inquire into what happened, or why children were running away, they were being flogged.**

As Secwépemc people, we are strong. We are a resilient family, born into a powerful culture and traditions. **We doubt that grandpa was buried with the dignity he deserves. He was a human being and deserved a proper burial.** We are engaged as a family in support of the search being done by Williams Lake First Nation. I am a part of the investigation team to find our children that disappeared. Through a combination of state of the art technology and the guidance of our traditions and ceremonies, we will do our best to find grandpa, and all other missing children and honor them as they should have been." [30]

CANADA'S APOLOGY

On June 11, 2008, former Prime Minister Stephen Harper issued a public apology for the role that the Canadian Government played in the Residential School System. Harper stood in the House of Commons and apologized. Here are some excerpts of that apology: [31]

"Mr. Speaker, I stand before you today to offer an apology to former students of Indian Residential Schools. The treatment of children in Indian Residential Schools is a sad chapter in our history. In the 1870s, the federal government, partly in order to meet its obligation to educate Aboriginal children, began to play a role in the development and administration of these schools.

...These objectives were based on the assumption Aboriginal cultures and spiritual beliefs were inferior and unequal. Indeed, some sought, as it was infamously said, `to kill the Indian in the child.' Today, we recognize that this policy of assimilation was wrong, has caused great harm, and has no place in our country.

...It has taken extraordinary courage for the thousands of Survivors that have come forward to speak publicly about the abuse they suffered.

...It is a testament to their resilience as individuals and to the strength of their cultures. Regrettably, many former students are not with us today and died never having received a full apology from the Government of Canada.

...Therefore, on behalf of the Government of Canada and all Canadians, I stand before you, in this chamber so central to our life as a country, to apologize to Aboriginal Peoples for Canada's role in the Indian Residential Schools System.

...There is no place in Canada for the attitudes that inspired the Indian Residential Schools System to ever again prevail."

ROYAL CANADIAN MOUNTED POLICE APOLOGY

During the operation of Indian Residential Schools, the RCMP assisted Indian Agents and the Department of Indian Affairs with various requests such as finding and returning students who had run away from school. Ultimately, the RCMP were used as a tool by the government to maintain the system.

In May of 2004, former RCMP Commissioner Giuliano Zaccardelli issued a public apology on behalf of the RCMP. He said,

"...To those of you who suffered tragedies at Residential Schools, we are very sorry for your experience. Canadians can never forget what happened and they never should. The RCMP is optimistic that we can all work together to learn from this Residential School system experience and ensure that it never happens again. We - I, as Commissioner of the RCMP - am truly sorry for what role we played in the Residential School system and the abuse that took place in that system." [32]

THE POPE'S APOLOGY

Kúkpi7 Rosanne Casimir, Golden Day Woman of Tk'emlúps te Secwepémc and Tribal Chief of the Secwépemc Nation Tribal Council shared her experience surrounding visiting the vatican and Pope Francis.

Kúkpi7 Rosanne Casimir of Tk'emlúps te Secwépemc pictured with the sun rising in the background, on the former Kamloops Indian Residential School grounds. Photo taken by Victoria Lynn Reeb on August 25, 2021.

"My heart is with all survivors and intergenerational survivors who carried the painful truths, their truths and it is with this visit that I carry the voices of generations of Indigenous peoples impacted by the sins of the Residential Schools. **This journey for me was to bring honor and dignity to the ones who did not come home** *and carry forth and deliver messages on behalf of the many who shared their anger, their frustration, and their hope for the delivery of their messages being heard.*

I truly appreciate and thank the British Columbia Assembly of First Nations (BCAFN) for allowing me to represent BC on this journey to the Vatican. **For me, to take this journey to the highest level of the Roman Catholic Church to the Holy See himself, Pope Francis was meaningful, impactful, and truly historical.** *I was part of a family that brought forth the impacts of the harms suffered by our survivors, their families, and communities that remain unresolved.*

*As a delegate on behalf of the BCAFN **I ensured to express the significance of Pope Francis's Canadian Papal visit to Turtle Island include First Nation communities impacted by unmarked graves and to have our survivors and intergenerational survivors' opportunity to witness a true meaningful apology from the harms of Residential School and meaningful steps to address the reparations still needed for real reconciliation.***

*I went there representing our people to the hope of building meaningful steps towards reconciliation while seeking justice in whatever forum our people seek through this very dark chapter in our history towards the renewal and rebuilding of relationships at every level; **this is a crucial time in history, and we all need to be a part of and witness true expressions of goodwill and meaningful steps forward.***

My hope is for reconciliation, and that reparations are mandated from the highest level so that we can truly walk together for our children and future generations, and that our remaining survivors and our intergenerational survivors bare witness to Pope Francis here on our Native lands where our families live to truly witness his address to our people and all those impacted from Indian Residential Schools that were run by the Roman Catholic Church.

I seek unity, peace, and hope for our people, our future generations as a leader, a mother, and a grandmother and an intergenerational survivor. I am Kúkpi7 Rosanne Casimir, Golden Day Woman of Tk'emlúps te Secwépemc and Tribal Chief of the Secwépemc Nation Tribal Council." [33]

In March 2022, First Nation, Métis and Inuit delegates visited The Vatican in Rome, Italy. They demanded an apology from the Pope and for the role the Catholic Church played in Residential Schools. In July of 2022, the Pope visited Canada and met with Residential School Survivors and their families as well as with Indigenous leaders and organizations. During that visit the Pope apologized using the following words:

*"I am sorry. I ask forgiveness, in particular, for the ways in which many members of the church and of religious communities co-operated, not least through their indifference, in projects of cultural destruction and forced assimilation promoted by the governments of that time, which culminated in the system of Residential Schools…**I humbly beg forgiveness for the evil committed by so many Christians against the Indigenous Peoples."*** [34]

Pope Francis told reporters on the flight back to Italy that ***"I didn't use the word genocide because it didn't come to mind but I described genocide."*** [35]

Although the Pope apologized for the behavior of how many Christians behaved, some believe that is not enough. Cindy Blackstock, a member of Gitksan First Nation and professor, stated:

*"The Pope apologized for the Catholic Church's role in Residential Schools. It was meaningful for some Residential School Survivors, and I am so grateful that it brought them some comfort. However, **when victims must travel to Rome to ask for an apology greater scrutiny is needed to ensure the apology delivers justice for the victims and is not just a proforma release of responsibility for the offender.** The Pope's apology began by recognizing the Governor General and the Prime Minister (which are both offices arising from colonialism) before mentioning the Residential School Survivors and the children who died to whom this apology is properly addressed. It talked about the future but was light on accountability and action and peppered with requests for God to forgive the Church. **The First Nations, Métis and Inuit children who attended residential schools and suffered so deeply and those who died there deserve […] more."*** [36]

RESILIENCE

The Residential School System set out to assimilate Indigenous people into mainstream society. Indigenous children were treated poorly, removed from their families and taught to feel worthless. Although these experiences created a lot of trauma in the Indigenous community, the Residential School system did not accomplish its goal. Indigenous languages, cultures, ceremonies and families are being revitalized because of the **resilience** of the people. [37]

Keisha Jones dancing at the 2019 Orange Shirt Day in Victoria, B.C. Photo taken by Eden Sunflower.

Keisha Jones dancing at the 2019 Orange Shirt Day in Victoria, B.C.:

*"My families Yakima lineage is where our connection to the powwow circle stems. It is through these lines that I have learned to dance. The style I practice is fancy shawl and represents the butterfly. I choose to dance in settings such as Orange Shirt Day to honour the lives lost at Residential Schools and the resilience in our communities. **I dance to inspire the young ones, show them how dancing can empower them in their identities and help heal their wounds. I dance to honour the spirits of those who have walked before us and those who have passed on.** I dance to lift the spirits of the Elders present and those who can no longer dance."* [38]

CHAPTER THREE QUESTIONS
REFLECTION ON LEARNING

1. Provide 5 of the "truths of what happened in Residential Schools" that are introduced in Chapter 3.
2. What is Chief Fred Robbins's vision of reconciliation? Explain why this might be important in order for reconciliation to truly happen.
3. In the quoted text, "When the school is on the reserve, the child lives with his parents who are savages; he is surrounded by savages... He is simply a savage who can read and write," to what extent do you think that John A Macdonald's words have affected and continue to affect Indigenous peoples in Canada?
4. Even though the records are incomplete, how many children are presumed to have not returned home from Residential School? Why is it hard to know exactly how many children attended?
5. During which years did government-sponsored Residential Schools run? Why is it important to understand this fact? In what ways might the timeframe that Residential Schools were open affect reconciliation efforts today?
6. What stands out for you when you see the map indicating the places where Residential Schools were located?
7. Why were many Residential Schools located in isolated areas? What impact did this have on the Indigenous children who attended these schools and their families? Why might this be important to consider today?
8. What were some things that happened to Indigenous children when they arrived and lived at Residential Schools? Why do you think their experience was different from other non-Indigenous children attending schools at the time?
9. Why were churches "eager to embrace" maintaining and running Residential Schools? How might this have affected Survivors and their families both in the short and long term?
10. Explain fully what things stood out to you from the description about St. Joseph's Mission Residential School.
11. What types of things from the Survivors' stories about their Residential School experience stood out to you? Explain fully.
12. What is intergenerational trauma? Are there Intergenerational Survivors alive today? Why do we need to consider Intergenerational trauma for reconciliation to happen?
13. Explain what you think is meant by the statement "so much is unsaid about some of the complications and challenges he experienced in his lifetime due to Residential School." Why is this important to consider in relation to reconciliation?
14. Explain what lateral violence is in relation to Residential School. To what extent and how might this affect the process of reconciliation?
15. Jeremy Boston shares "the past is something that cannot be erased but can be healed through education and knowledge ... your voice is powerful. Learn to forgive and move forward." How does this idea apply to all peoples living in Canada?
16. The National Centre for Truth and Reconciliation stated "there is a common theme of 'how could this happen?' in the questions raised. The answer is complex, rooted in racism and unjust policies." When you reflect on the stories of Survivors and images shared, to what degree do you think this statement is accurate and why/why not?
17. Why do you think that it was not required for the deaths of Indigenous children attending Residential Schools to be recorded or there to be any inquiry into why they died or why they were running away from schools? What does this reveal about the way Indigenous peoples were viewed in Canada?
18. What do you think it was like for children, some as young as two, four and six-years-old, who were forced to leave their families and attend Residential Schools for the first time? How do you think those children felt being forced to leave their families and communities?
19. Why do you think we refer to Residential School Survivors and Intergenerational Survivors as "Survivors" instead of victims. How could the choice of words affect their journey?
20. Why do you think it was important for Canada, the RCMP, and the Pope to each apologize for their part in Residential Schools? After reading the words in each apology, what stands out for you? How might this help to move forward the process of reconciliation?
 What do you think the purpose was behind students being given numbers in place of their names while attending Residential
21. Schools? How might being a number affect one's sense of belonging and self?

RESEARCH

1. Do you know if there was a Residential School in your area? Can you name the school? Do you know anyone who attended the school?
2. Find a book that details the personal accounts of Indigenous people who attended Residential Schools. Ask your librarian or a teacher for help or visit our website for more resources at www.medicinewheel.education/orangeshirtday
   What stands out most for you in their story?
3. Look up St. Joseph's Mission Indian Residential School definition. Take note of the different names of the Residential School. One of those names is Williams Lake Industrial School. Research why the word 'Industrial' was used in reference to Residential School.
4. Do some research to find out the reason that some children ran away from Residential Schools? Hint: research Chanie Wenjack.
5. Do some research to find out what happened to many Indigenous Residential School students who spoke in their traditional languages or practiced their cultural customs?
6. Look up to find out other nations that had systems similar to Canada's Residential School System. How were they similar? How were they different?

SOURCES

1. "Truth and Reconciliation Commissions: By the Numbers." CBC News. Daniel Schwartz. June 2, 2015. <https://www.cbc.ca/news/indigenous/truth-and-reconciliation-commission-by-the-numbers-1.3096185> accessed May 28, 2020.
2. "Truth and Reconciliation Commissions: By the Numbers." CBC News. Daniel Schwartz. June 2, 2015. <https://www.cbc.ca/news/indigenous/truth-and-reconciliation-commission-by-the-numbers-1.3096185> accessed May 28, 2020.
3. "Work to exhume remains at former Kamloops residential school could begin soon, chief says". CBC News. Dirk Meissner.<https://www.cbc.ca/news/canada/british-columbia/tk-eml%C3%BAps-kamloops-indian-residential-school-215-exhumations-1.6460796>. Accessed November 30th, 2022.
   "The History of Native American Boarding Schools Is Even More Complicated than a New Report Reveals". Time Magazine. Olivia Waxman. <https://time.com/6177069/american-indian-boarding-schools-history/> accessed November 30th, 2022.
4. "Truth and Reconciliation Commissions: By the Numbers." CBC News. Daniel Schwartz. June 2, 2015. <https://www.cbc.ca/news/indigenous/truth-and-reconciliation-commission-by-the-numbers-1.3096185> accessed May 28, 2020.
5. "10 Quotes John A. Macdonald Made About First Nations." Indigenous Corporate Training. June 28, 2016. < https://www.ictinc.ca/blog/10-quotes-john-a.-macdonald-made-about-rst-nations > accessed May 28, 2020.
6. "Indian Residential Schools and Reconciliation: 1920-1927 Indian Act Becomes More Restrictive." First Nations Education Steering Committee. <http://www.fnesc.ca/wp/wp-content/uploads/2015/07/IRSR11-12-DE-1920-1927.pdf> accessed May 28, 2020.
7. Webstad, Phyllis. Joan Sorley, Tiany Moses and Harold Tarbell. St. Joseph's Mission Residential School Commemoration Project Booklet. Remembering, Recovering, and Reconciling. Williams Lake: Tarbell Facilitation Network, 2013. pp. 6.
8. The Truth and Reconciliation Commission of Canada. They Came for the Children. Manitoba: Library and Archives Canada Cataloguing in Publication, 2012. pp. 22.
9. The Truth and Reconciliation Commission of Canada. They Came for the Children. Manitoba: Library and Archives Canada Cataloguing in Publication, 2012. pp. 30, 34, 41, 44.
   "Residential Schools in Canada." The Canadian Encyclopedia. January 15, 2020. < https://www.thecanadianencyclopedia.ca/en/article/residential-schools#LifeatResidentialSchools> accessed June 1, 2020.
10. "Canada's Residential Schools: The History, Part 1 Origins to 1939." Truth and Reconciliation Commission of Canada. 2015. <http://www.trc.ca/assets/pdf/Volume_1_History_Part_1_English_Web.pdf> accessed May 30, 2020. pp. 337.
11. The Truth and Reconciliation Commission of Canada. They Came for the Children. Manitoba: Library and Archives Canada Cataloguing in Publication, 2012. pp. 18.
12. The Truth and Reconciliation Commission of Canada. They Came for the Children. Manitoba: Library and Archives Canada Cataloguing in Publication, 2012. pp. 10.
13. The Truth and Reconciliation Commission of Canada. They Came for the Children. Manitoba: Library and Archives Canada Cataloguing in Publication, 2012. pp. 13.
14. Webstad, Phyllis. Joan Sorley, Tiany Moses and Harold Tarbell. St. Joseph's Mission Residential School Commemoration Project Booklet. Remembering, Recovering, and Reconciling. Williams Lake: Tarbell Facilitation Network, 2013. pp. 4-5.
15. Wilson, Nee Jack, Rose. Beyond the Orange Shirt Story. Medicine Wheel Education. Victoria. Printed in PRC. September 1st, 2021. P. 40, 41.
16. Webstad, Phyllis. The Orange Shirt Story. Medicine Wheel Education, Victoria. Printed: PRC. September 1, 2018.
17. Webstad, Phyllis. Joan Sorley, Tiany Moses and Harold Tarbell. St. Joseph's Mission Residential School Commemoration Project Booklet. Remembering, Recovering, and Reconciling. Williams Lake: Tarbell Facilitation Network, 2013. pp. 6.
18. "Chief Ann Louie Speech." Boitanio Park Monument Unveiling. The Commemoration Project Events. Filmed by John Dell. Signal Point Media, 2013. DVD.
19. "The Intergenerational Trauma of First Nations Still Run Deep." The Global and Mail. Kevin Berube. February 16, 2015. <https://www.theglobeandmail.com/life/health-and-tness/health-advisor/the-intergenerational-trauma-of-rst-nations-still-runs-deep/article23013789/> accessed May 24, 2020.
20. "The Intergenerational Trauma of First Nations Still Run Deep." The Global and Mail. Kevin Berube. February 16, 2015. <https://www.theglobeandmail.com/life/health-and-tness/health-advisor/the-intergenerational-trauma-of-rst-nations-still-runs-deep/article23013789/> accessed May 24, 2020.
21. Harvey, Karlene. Personal Interview. April. 2020.
22. "Intergenerational Survivors." Where are the Children. November 28, 2013. <http://wherearethechildren.ca/en/watc_blackboard/intergenerational-survivors/> accessed May 10, 2020.
23. "Intervention to address Intergenerational Trauma." <https://www.ucalgary.ca/wethurston/les/wethurston/Report_InterventionToAddressIntergenerationalTrauma.pdf> accessed May 1, 2020.
24. Webstad, Phyllis. Personal Interview. March, 2023.
25. Boston, Jeremy. Beyond the Orange Shirt Story. Medicine Wheel Education. Victoria. Printed in PRC. September 1st, 2021. P. 65-68.
26. "Grief, sorrow after discovery of 215 bodies, unmarked graves at former B.C. residential school site." Global News. Potente, Doyle. <https://globalnews.ca/news/7902306/unmarked-graves-kamloops-residential-school/> accessed November 30th, 2022.
27. "'This is heavy truth': Tk'emlúps te Secwépemc chief says more to be done to identify unmarked graves." CBC news. Sterritt, Angela & Dickson, Courtney. <https://www.cbc.ca/news/canada/british-columbia/kamloops-residential-school-findings-1.6084185. Accessed November 30th, 2022.
28. "215 Innocent Children. National Centre for Truth and Reconciliation. Scott, Stephanie. <https://nctr.ca/215-innocent-children/> accessed November 30th, 2022.
29. "St. Joseph's Mission Investigation." Williams Lake First Nation. <https://www.wlfn.ca/chief-council/sjm-investigation-releases-2/#:~:text=WLFN%20has%20used%20Ground%20Penetrating,Joseph's%20Mission> accessed February, 2023.
30. Belleau, Charlene. Personal Interview. February, 2023.
31. "Text of Stephen Harper's Residential Schools Apology." CTV News. The Canadian Press. June 11, 2008. <https://www.ctvnews.ca/text-of-stephen-harper-s-residential-schools-apology-1.301820> accessed January, 2020.
32. "Indian Residential School apologies." Royal Canadian Mounted Police. November 29, 2019. <https://www.rcmp-grc.gc.ca/aboriginal-autochtone/apo-reg-eng.htm> Accessed April 20, 2020.
33. Kukpi7 Casimir, Rosanne (Golden Day Woman). Tkemlups te Secwepemc and Tribal Chief of the Secwepemc Nation Tribal Council. Personal Interview. March, 2023.
34. "'I am deeply sorry': Full text of residential school apology from Pope Francis". The Canadian Press. <"https://www.cbc.ca/news/canada/edmonton/pope-francis-maskwacis-apology-full-text-1.6531341>. Accessed March 15th, 2023.
35. "Pope says genocide took place at Canada's residential schools" CBC News. <https://www.cbc.ca/news/indigenous/pope-francis-residential-schools-genocide-1.6537203#:~:text=%22I%20didn't%20use%20the,Iqaluit%20to%20Rome%20on%20Friday> Accessed March 14th, 2023.
36. "Expert: Pope Francis apologizes for forced assimilation of Indigenous children at residential schools." Media Relations, McGill UniversityPublished: July, 2022. <https://www.mcgill.ca/newsroom/channels/news/expert-pope-francis-apologizes-forced-assimilation-indigenous-children-residential-schools-340476> accessed November 30th, 2023.
37. Webstad, Phyllis. Personal Interview. January, 2020.
38. Jones, Keisha. Personal Interview. May, 2020.

CHAPTER

4 ORANGE SHIRT DAY
AND THE ORANGE SHIRT SOCIETY

Orange Shirt Day is a legacy of the St. Joseph's Mission Residential School Commemoration Project. Since its creation, Orange Shirt Day has become a movement that inspires Indian Residential School reconciliation and has created safe spaces for Survivors, and their families, to bravely share their experiences.

Orange Shirt Day acknowledges the Residential School tragedies and, in turn, creates opportunities for collective and individual healing, recovery and reconciliation. Since the first Orange Shirt Day, on September 30, 2013, many people have begun to awaken to this shameful chapter in our history and the importance of establishing a new legacy for Indigenous people that says, "Every Child Matters."

Shawn Atleo, former National Assembly of First Nations Chief from 2009 to 2014, at the first Orange Shirt Day in 2013 at Boitanio Park in Williams Lake. Photo courtesy of the Williams Lake CRD.

THE MOMENT THE SEED FOR ORANGE SHIRT DAY WAS PLANTED

As part of the commemorative events a Residential School Survivor's reunion was being planned by a committee. That committee asked Phyllis Webstad to represent their group at the April 23, 2013, press conference to kick off the week of events. Phyllis was nervous about speaking and didn't know what she was going to say. Phyllis asked her friend, who was also working on the St. Joseph's Mission Commemoration Project, to meet for coffee and discuss her upcoming speech.

Residential School Survivor Phyllis Webstad, School District #27 Superintendent Mark Thiessen, Chair of the Cariboo CRD Al Richmond, Former Williams Lake Mayor Kerry Cook and Chief Fred Robbins at the press conference promoting St. Joseph's Mission Commemoration Project in 2013 at Boitanio Park in Williams Lake. Photo taken by Monica Lamb-Yorski of the Williams Lake Tribune.

"*I met my friend at the Bean Counter, a local coffee shop. My friend and I were to meet and discuss what I would say at the press conference the next morning, I was very nervous. My friend could only meet later in the day, so at like 4:15 or so we decided to meet. My friend was already there. I stood in line for my coffee and by the time I was sitting down I knew what I would talk about the next day. I get choked up everytime I tell this part. **I sat down and told my friend I knew what I was going to talk about, my first day at Residential School. I immediately had tears streaming down my face and told my friend the story.***

When I finished, I realized I had nothing orange in my closet and that I needed to get shopping. By this time it was close to five and stores in Williams Lake close by six so I didn't have much time. I went to my favorite women's clothing store. I couldn't find an orange shirt but I did find an orange mesh sweater, so I bought that and that's what I wore. In the photo of us in the park you can see all the people with titles, Chief, Superintendent, Mayor, CRD Chair then there's me, unemployed Residential School Survivor... in bright orange!"

- Phyllis Webstad[1]

In Williams Lake in 2013, Phyllis Webstad shared her story about her orange shirt publicly for the first time. Photo taken by Monica Lamb-Yorski of the Williams Lake Tribune.

At the press conference, for the first time, Phyllis Webstad publicly spoke about her story of her orange shirt and her experience attending Residential School. This is what Phyllis had to say:

*My name is Phyllis Webstad... **I went to St. Joseph's when I had just turned six in 1973-1974. I just went for one year... I'm the third generation.** My grandmother went for ten years... my mother went and I went... My grandmother probably couldn't afford it but she always bought a new set of clothes for all the kids going to the Mission and I was no exception. **It was really exciting. I picked out an orange shirt and it was really shiny and it just sparkled... When I got there we got stripped... my orange shirt was taken away... To me orange has never been my friend. So I wear it today as a symbol of the healing that is taking place.** Orange has always been to me... not mattering to anyone, nobody cared that we had feelings... just being insignificant. So to me that's what orange means. Today, that's why I wear it. That's not the case anymore.*

- Phyllis Webstad[2]

For Phyllis, sharing her story was not an easy decision as her experience at Residential School had impacted her entire life.

Phyllis explained how difficult it was to wear the colour orange. The colour brought up feelings of low self-worth due to the trauma she experienced as a child at Residential School. *"As a result, orange came to symbolize for her that nobody cared that she had feelings and that she just didn't matter and how it led to her growing up thinking she wasn't worth anything."* [3] Phyllis's orange shirt represents the triumphant reclamation of her identity, self worth and hope for the future.

Many other Survivors connect with her story because they too had similar experiences of their identity and belongings being taken away. Ultimately, Phyllis's story is a conversation starter about all aspects of Residential Schools and the way that the system negatively affected individuals and families, both first-hand and generationally.

Phyllis' story was so powerful and relatable, not only to other Survivors and their families, but to everyone. Many felt it greatly represented not only the trauma inflicted by Residential Schools but also the pain felt afterwards and the long journey of healing and recovery.

The commemoration project started as a vision for reconciliation from Chief Fred Robbins. Chief Fred's vision was to put an epitaph in the form of a monument to remember those children who did not survive Residential School, including those who died later as a result of their traumatic experiences. He knew he could not do it alone and reached out to the community for support. Community members rallied around Chief Fred's vision of the reconciliation monuments which blossomed into the St. Joseph's Mission Residential School Commemoration Project.

The commemoration project planning committee included, Chief Fred Robbins, Jerome Beauchamp (School District 27), Anne Burrill (City of Williams Lake), Eric Chrona (Royal Canadian Mounted Police), Joan Sorley (Cariboo Regional District), Rick Gilbert (Williams Lake Indian Band), David DeRose (School District 27), late Phillip Robbins, Tiffany Moses (mentored youth), Harold Tarbell (Tarbell Facilitation Network), and Phyllis Webstad (Residential School Survivor).

At the time of the commemoration project events in 2013, Kerry Cook was the Mayor of Williams Lake. Chief Fred consulted with Kerry to get the city of Williams Lake involved in the process of reconciliation. Kerry was inspired by Chief Fred, his vision and his passion to create change. She didn't hesitate to become involved.

Chief Fred Robbins' passion to bring Indigenous and non-Indigenous people together to acknowledge the painful truths of Residential Schools and begin the recovery process had become a reality that inspired national change and healing for many. The Orange Shirt Society thanks Chief Fred for starting the community on a path to reconciliation.

ST. JOSEPH'S MISSION COMMEMORATIVE MONUMENTS

There were many events that took place during the week-long commemoration project. The Orange Shirt Society would like to highlight the ceremonies where two commemorative 'brother and sister' monuments were raised. *"Two monuments are dedicated: one at the site of St. Joseph's Mission School to memorialize the former students and the other in Boitanio park in Williams Lake to jointly commit to shared reconciliation. Both monuments contain excerpts from Prime Minister Stephen Harper's and the Oblates of Mary Immaculate's official apologies."* [4] Communities from near and far came to both ceremonies to honour the former students and their families.

> *So here we are, the city of Williams Lake, the First Nations in and around. The 15 bands. We stand here in front of, hopefully, a new legacy.* **Creating a future for our children.** *'Every Child Matters,' as the National Chief stated.* **Every Child Matters.** *It's that next generation that we have to start teaching. We are at all different levels as Residential School Survivors, all different levels of healing... A lot of parents forgot how to parent [and] grandparents forgot how to be grandparents.* **We need to start creating a new legacy, and it starts within the communities. It starts with the communities... Let's recognize that together as a people, not as First Nations and non-First Nations but as a people... that's how we have to do this...**
>
> - Chief Fred Robbins[5]

During the monument ceremonies, and other events, there were signs of Orange Shirt Day already. People were wearing "Every Child Matters" pins, the choir wore orange scarves and the committee handed out orange bags. It was a sign that Orange Shirt Day would become the medium for continuing the conversation about Residential Schools annually.

Musicians Gary Fjellgaard and Murray Porter each shared the songs they wrote after hearing Canada's 2008 federal apology for the Residential School System. Gary performed his song '*I Apologize*', and Murray performed his song '*Is Sorry Enough*' during the commemoration project events.

Monument at the site of St. Joseph's Mission Residential School. Photo by Teddy Anderson.

THE FIRST ORANGE SHIRT DAY

After Phyllis shared her story at the press conference in April of 2013, the idea for Orange Shirt Day was born. After all events were completed around the St. Joseph's Mission Residential School Commemoration Project, the planning committee morphed into the Orange Shirt Society.

> *The annual Orange Shirt Day on September 30th opens the door to global conversation on all aspects of Residential Schools.* ***It is an opportunity to create meaningful discussion about the effects of Residential Schools and the legacy they have left behind.*** *A discussion all Canadians can tune into and create bridges with each other for reconciliation. A day for survivors to be reaffirmed that they matter, and so do those that have been affected. Every Child Matters, even if they are an adult, from now on.*
>
> - Phyllis Webstad[6]

As word about Phyllis's story and Orange Shirt Day began to spread, people wanted to become involved and begin walking the path of reconciliation. Prior to the first Orange Shirt Day, Shannon Bell, a pastor in the community of Ndazkoh B.C., witnessed Phyllis share her orange shirt story at a TRC event in May of 2013. She was inspired by Phyllis's courage and recognized the importance of creating momentum for Orange Shirt Day. Shannon quickly took action to become involved and share Phyllis's story.

The very first Orange Shirt Day was on September 30th, 2013 and events were held across Canada and beyond. At these events, Indigenous and non-Indigenous local communities came together to support the creation of a new legacy for Indigenous peoples.

The first Orange Shirt Day turned out to be much bigger than initially expected. The day was organized by Phyllis Webstad, David DeRose, Joan Sorley, Jerome Beauchamp, and Anne Burrill for the Williams Lake and 100 Mile House communities. Today, Orange Shirt Day has spread to a massive movement with millions of people, Indigenous and non-Indigenous, walking together toward a path of reconciliation.

Lucy Squalian and carver Dean Gilpin pose in front of one of the commemorative monuments, showing Dean's artwork, in Williams Lake. Photo is by Valerie West.

WHY SEPTEMBER 30th

The date of September 30th was chosen very carefully. This date represented the time of year when the Indigenous children were collected from their homes, forced to leave their families and attend Residential Schools. September 30th was chosen to allow schools and teachers to settle into their school year, teach the students about Residential Schools and to plan an event for Orange Shirt Day. Additionally, by having Orange Shirt Day at the beginning of the school year, it sets the stage for anti-racism and anti-bullying policies to inspire inclusion.

"While listening to the truths at the September, 2013, TRC event in Vancouver I overheard an Elder say that September was crying month. It was then that I knew that we had chosen the right day for Orange Shirt Day."

- Phyllis Webstad [7]

WHY THE MESSAGE "EVERY CHILD MATTERS"

"Every Child Matters" is the chosen theme and one of the core guiding principles for the Orange Shirt Society. It was chosen in response to Phyllis feeling that she did not matter. This message reminds Survivors that they are important and they matter. "Every Child Matters" extends beyond Residential School Survivors and their families, to include all children. "Every Child Matters" also includes those children who died at, or as a result of, Residential Schools.

"Every Child Matters" is for all children past, present and future. All children in Canada and beyond. All those who were children. All those who suffered as children at Residential School who became adults and those that didn't. When the Orange Shirt Society says "Every Child Matters"… it means everyone, including you who are reading this, regardless of background or age.

ORANGE SHIRT DAY AND INTERGENERATIONAL TRAUMA

Orange Shirt Day has inspired many people and events to honour Residential School Survivors, their families and the children who didn't come home. Through this day, and the movement towards reconciliation that it has inspired, people are beginning to understand and acknowledge the painful truths that have impacted individuals, families and communities.

By sharing the effects of Phyllis Webstad's intergenerational trauma, Phyllis has shown us how difficult it is to overcome the long-lasting pain caused by Residential Schools. One of the most powerful outcomes of Orange Shirt Day is that it has inspired people to share their first-hand and intergenerational experiences with Residential Schools.

*I was 13.8 years old and in grade eight when my son Jeremy was born. **Because my grandmother and mother both attended Residential School for ten years each, I never knew what a parent was supposed to be like.** With the help of my aunt, Agness Jack, I was able to raise my son and have him know me as his mother.*

*I went to a treatment centre for healing when I was 27 and have been on this healing journey since then. I finally get it, that the feeling of worthlessness and insignificance, ingrained in me from my first day at the Mission, affected the way I lived my life for many years. **Even now, when I know nothing could be further than the truth, I still sometimes feel that I don't matter. Even with all the work I've done!***

-Phyllis Webstad[8]

These shared stories have emphasized a collective truth amongst Indigenous peoples that can no longer be ignored. Through the acknowledgement of these shared truths, the process of healing and recovery can be widely embraced creating reconciliation among Indigenous and non-Indigenous people.

Phyllis Webstad reading from her book Phyllis's Orange Shirt at Orange Shirt Day 2019 in Williams Lake. Photo by Monica Lamb-Yorski of the Williams Lake Tribune

Nanestsen (I care for you)

"*In this image, I depict a contemporary young First Nations woman holding a girl in a Residential School uniform, she holds her close in a way that conveys both love and protection. The girl's hair is short due to mandatory regulations at Residential School that forced children to have their hair cut. The young woman has kept her hair long and braided and while she's dressed in contemporary fashion she also chooses to wear moccasins and beaded earrings.* **I wanted to show that First Nations and Indigenous people have endured the harm experienced at Residential Schools through multi-generational resilience. As time moves forward, we remain tethered to our ancestors who experienced this harm and I wonder about the space, compassion and understanding we can share with our relations both in the present and our past.**"*

Artwork by Karlene Harvey. [9]

THE ORANGE SHIRT SOCIETY

The Orange Shirt Society is a non-profit organization created by a group of volunteers, from the St. Joseph's Mission Commemoration Project, who are committed to the development of Orange Shirt Day. The Society is located in Williams Lake B.C., where Phyllis Webstad first shared her story about her orange shirt and attended St. Joseph's Mission Residential School. The Society was formed as a way to organize Orange Shirt Day, create events and spread awareness. Orange Shirt Society has three purposes that aid in the development and awareness of Orange Shirt Day: [7]

- To support Indian Residential School Reconciliation
- To create awareness of the individual, family and community intergenerational impacts of Indian Residential Schools through Orange Shirt Society activities
- To create awareness of the concept of "Every Child Matters"

The Orange Shirt Society is directed by a board of both Indigenous and non-Indigenous volunteers. The founding members of the Orange Shirt Society are Phyllis Webstad, David DeRose, Joan Sorley, Jerome Beauchamp, Margo Wagner, Margaret Anne-Enders and Anne Burrill.

It took Phyllis nearly 40 years to wear the colour orange again after the Residential School took away her orange shirt. Now she, and the Orange Shirt Society, have bravely transformed her painful experience into a movement that represents Residential School reconciliation and healing. What was once a symbol of pain and tragedy for Phyllis, is now a symbol of hope. Phyllis now wears orange shirts to symbolize that "Every Child Matters," including her and you.

You too can wear an orange shirt on September 30th to send the message that "Every Child Matters." Wearing orange also shows that you acknowledge and support the healing journey of Indigenous people who are courageously recovering from the effects of Residential Schools and building a new legacy for themselves, their families, and communities.

The government that did this to us will never go to jail for what they did. Whenever I see someone wearing an orange shirt and witness children in schools learning about what happened to us, it feels like a little bit of justice in our lifetime.

- Phyllis Webstad [10]

Phyllis Webstad admiring student artwork at Desert Sands Community School, Ashcroft, B.C. presentation in 2019.

ORANGE SHIRT DAY AND THE NATIONAL DAY FOR TRUTH AND RECONCILIATION

Orange Shirt Day has expanded across Canada and beyond. Initially envisioned as an opportunity to hold tough conversations about what happened in Residential Schools in the Cariboo Region of British Columbia, it has now become a widely recognized movement for reconciliation. Orange Shirt Day is not only a day to honour Survivors, their families and the children who did not make it home, but it is also an opportunity for people of all ages and backgrounds to become educated about Residential Schools and the process of reconciliation while promoting "Every Child Matters."

For many years, Phyllis Webstad and other Orange Shirt Society board members have advocated to the government to establish Orange Shirt Day, taking place on September 30th, as a National Day for Truth and Reconciliation per recommendation #80 put forth by the Truth and Reconciliation Commission. The recommendation stated:

*"**We call upon the federal government, in collaboration with Aboriginal peoples, to establish, as a statutory holiday, a National Day for Truth and Reconciliation to honour Survivors, their families, and communities**, and ensure that public commemoration of the history and legacy of Residential Schools remains a vital component of the reconciliation process."* [11]

Today, millions of Canadians from all backgrounds are participating in Orange Shirt Day – National Day for Truth and Reconciliation. Justin Trudeau, Prime Minister of Canada stated:

"It is our shared responsibility to confront the legacy of residential schools and the ongoing impacts on Indigenous Peoples, so we can truly move forward together. That is why, last year, Parliament voted unanimously to establish the National Day for Truth and Reconciliation as an opportunity for all Canadians to learn more, honour the Survivors of residential schools, their families, and their communities, and remember the many children who never returned home. ***Reconciliation is not the responsibility of Indigenous Peoples – it is the responsibility of all Canadians. It is our responsibility to continue to listen and to learn.****"*

- Justin Trudeau [12]

EVERY CHILD MATTERS!!

Children marching for Orange Shirt Day in Shulus, B.C. Photo taken by Dara Hill of the Merritt Herald

CHAPTER FOUR QUESTIONS
REFLECTION ON LEARNING

1. What are some of the effects Phyllis Webstad had after sharing her story at the press conference in April 2013?

2. Phyllis Webstad mentioned that she was not the first generation of people from her family to attend a Residential School. How many generations of her family attended Residential Schools?

3. In May, 2013, there was a series of reconciliation events that took place. Who did it involve and what was the main goal? Where did these events take place?

4. What date was chosen to be Orange Shirt Day? Why was this date chosen?

5. Who is the Orange Shirt Society referring to when they say "Every Child Matters?"

6. Fill in the blank. What was once a symbol of pain and tragedy for Phyllis, is now a symbol of _____.

7. An orange shirt has become a symbol. What do you think it symbolizes for Indigenous Survivors of Residential Schools, like Phyllis Webstad? Please write what you think it symbolizes to those affected in your own words.

8. What do you think are appropriate terms to use when referring to Orange Shirt Day? Celebrate? Honour? Remember? Which do you think is honouring the day appropriately considering the context of the Orange Shirt Day?

RESEARCH

1. In what ways and to what extent have the efforts made by Chief Fred Robbins, the planning committee, and the St. Joseph Mission Residential School Commemoration Project begun to create a new legacy that has gained momentum for reconciliation between Indigenous and non-Indigenous peoples in Canada?

2. Chief Fred's goal for this project was reconciliation. Why do you think he needed both Indigenous and non-Indigenous people to participate in order to achieve reconciliation?

3. What types of things are being done across Canada to honour Orange Shirt Day – National Day for Truth and Reconciliation? What might you do to support this movement?

4. Research to find other Indigenous and non-Indigenous people who have used writing or art to share their experiences with the process of reconciliation. Which of these stands out for you? Why do you think it does?

ACTIVITY

Write a letter to all Canadians answering the following questions:

- Briefly answer what took place in the Residential School system in Canada.
- Why should all Canadians be concerned with Indigenous rights?
- Explain Phyllis's story to them and why her story is important for all Canadians to understand.
- What would the future of the world look like if every child were treated like they mattered?

SOURCES

1. Webstad, Phyllis. Personal Interview. January. 2020
2. Phyllis Webstad Shares her Orange Shirt Story for the First Time." Commemoration Project Event Press Conference. Filmed by John Dell. Signal Point Media, 2013. Film.
3. Tarbell, Harold. St. Joseph's Mission Residential School Commemoration Project Document. Remembering, Recovering, and Reconciling. Williams Lake: Tarbell Facilitation Network, 2013.
4. Webstad, Phyllis. Joan Sorley, Tiany Moses and Harold Tarbell. St. Joseph's Mission Residential School Commemoration Project Booklet. Remembering, Recovering, and Reconciling. Williams Lake: Tarbell Facilitation Network, 2013. pp. 12.
5. Tarbell, Harold. St. Joseph's Mission Residential School Commemoration Project Document. Remembering, Recovering, and Reconciling. Williams Lake: Tarbell Facilitation Network, 2013.
6. Webstad, Phyllis. Personal Interview. January. 2020.
7. Webstad, Phyllis. Personal Interview. January. 2020.
8. Webstad, Phyllis. Personal Interview. January. 2020.
9. Harvey, Karlene. Personal Interview. April. 2020.
10. Webstad, Phyllis. Personal Interview. January. 2020.
11. "Truth and Reconciliation Commission of Canada: Calls to Action" <https://www2.gov.bc.ca/assets/gov/british-columbians-our-governments/indigenous-people/aboriginal-peoples-documents/calls_to_action_english2.pdf> accessed March 6th, 2023.
12. Statement by the Prime Minister on the National Day for Truth and Reconciliation". Government of Canada. <https://pm.gc.ca/en/news/statements/2022/09/30/statement-prime-minister-national-day-truth-and-reconciliation#:~:text=The%20experiences%20and%20intergenerational%20trauma,can%20truly%20move%20forward%20together> accessed March 16th, 2023.

Student artwork from Langdale Elementary school. Photo courtesy of Duncan Knight.

CHAPTER

5 PARTICIPATING IN ORANGE SHIRT DAY
& A NATIONAL DAY FOR TRUTH AND RECONCILIATION

Participating in Orange Shirt Day on September 30th can motivate massive and positive change collectively, nationally and individually. Through your participation you will contribute to creating a new legacy for Indigenous peoples. Your participation can include becoming educated on the history of Residential Schools in Canada and reconciliation as well as holding space for Survivors and their families to share their truths. Your participation and education will also help you to confront **racism**, stereotypes and prejudices against Indigenous people. Orange Shirt Day has the power to create a more inclusive future by inspiring reconciliation, broader education, new perspectives and societal change.

Orange Shirt Day is not just a day on September 30th, it is a year-around educational movement designed to raise awareness of the continuing impacts of Residential School and promote reconciliation. By participating and becoming an advocate for this movement, you are changing culture on local, national and personal levels. By investing your time, energy and resources into Orange Shirt Day you are creating a more educated, supportive and inclusive environment that truly believes "Every Child Matters."

There are many ways that you can participate in Orange Shirt Day. There is no limit on your involvement when it comes to creating a positive and rightful new legacy for Indigenous peoples. As you become educated on the history and pain of Residential Schools, you may also create new and groundbreaking ways to participate in Orange Shirt Day.

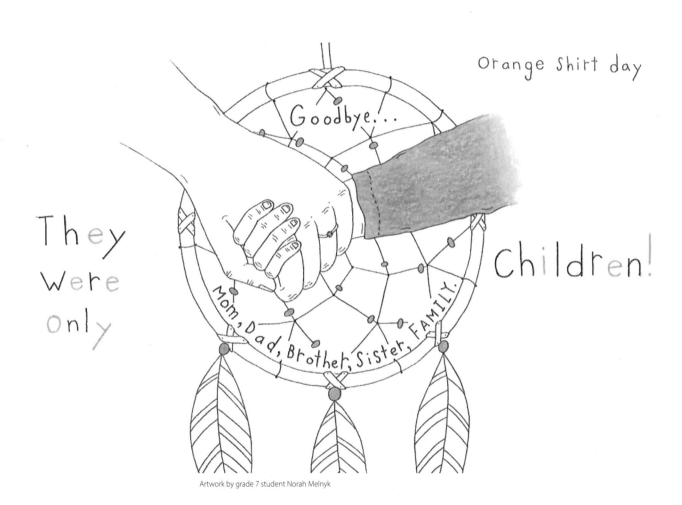

Artwork by grade 7 student Norah Melnyk

WEARING AN ORANGE SHIRT

The most obvious way to participate in Orange Shirt Day is to wear an orange shirt on September 30th! You can buy an official shirt through the the Orange Shirt Society's website at *www.orangeshirtday.org* where a portion of the proceeds go back to the Society.

It is important to know where your Orange Shirt Day shirt is coming from. Before you buy, be sure to research who is making the shirt. Is it from an Indigenous creator? An Indigenous-led organization? And do the funds go back to the Orange Shirt Society and other causes that support Residential School Survivors and their families?

Get creative with your own designs!

Those wanting to design their own shirts are encouraged to do so. Feel free to put a design on an orange shirt that means something to you or your Nation, but please be sure to use our slogan, Every Child Matters. You also may want to wear an orange bandana, scarf, button, (or whatever else you like) and those can be fun to design, too!

Creating your own orange shirt can be a great and social way to participate in Orange Shirt Day. You could make one on your own while reflecting on the reasons for your participation, or you could create one with friends and family while discussing your participation in reconciliation.

Whether you choose to make your orange shirt or purchase it, there are a couple of things to consider. It is important that your orange shirt says "Every Child Matters" because it's central to the purpose of Orange Shirt Society. If you don't have an orange shirt, can't afford one, or don't want to write on your shirt, anything orange will do! It's the conversation that's important.

Vancity staff pose for Orange Shirt Day 2018. Vancity is a founding partner of Reconciliation Canada. Photo taken by Paulina Tsui.

HOW TO SHARE PHYLLIS WEBSTAD'S STORY

Phyllis Webstad's hope is that you will share the story of her orange shirt and begin to educate yourself, and others, on Residential Schools and the experiences of Indigenous peoples. You can learn about Phyllis's story in this book, online, or through many other books created by Phyllis Webstad. The following are Phyllis's books, along with their appropriate ages:

Every Child Matters
English | French
Ages 7+
To be released in September 2023

With Our Orange Hearts
English | French
Ages 3-5
Illustrated by Emily Kewageshig
Best-selling children's book in Canada in September 2022

The Orange Shirt Story
English | French | Shuswap
Ages 7+
Best-selling children's book in Canada in September 2018

Phyllis's Orange Shirt
English | French
Ages 4-6
BC Best Seller in September 2019

Beyond the Orange Shirt Story
English | French
Ages 16+
BC Best Seller September 2021

Kamisha Alexson at an Orange Shirt Day event in Toronto 2019. Photo taken by Nadya Kwandibens of Red Works Photography.

BECOME AN ALLY

Becoming an ally, supporting Indigenous Peoples, and reconciliation is not an easy task to undertake. According to Amnesty International, *"Being a genuine ally involves a lot of self-reflection, education and listening. It means knowing we're often coming into this space from a position of power and privilege. **Privilege that we've gained through unjust systems that marginalize the groups we seek to ally with.** It's not enough to show up in solidarity and speak out against the unjust system, we have to do what is within our power to dismantle the system and differentiate ourselves from the opponents of these groups. We have to change our own behaviors and be mindful that we are not contributing to keeping that system going."* [1]

Bringing this concept into the context of allyship in truth and reconciliation, it is important to recognize your power and privilege. If you are non-Indigenous, standing in solidarity with Indigenous Peoples is critical to being an ally, while also seeking to dismantle the systems that grant you that privilege. If you are Indigenous, you can be an ally, too, by standing with other Indigenous Survivors and their families, encouraging healing and cooperation.

Amnesty International lists what being an ally should look like. It offers the following powerful self-reflection tools:

1.) **Listen to and follow the community**
Find out who the traditional owners and Elders are of the land you are on. When doing long-term work on Indigenous rights, build strong relationships within the community and make sure everything is First Nations-led.

2.) **Centre the stories around community**
A big part of your involvement is to amplify the voices of First Nations communities, don't make it about yourself. You should directly share these messages with your networks in their words without alteration.

3.) **Learn the historical and cultural context**
Knowing the history and being culturally competent is vital. The issues the community face come from hundreds of years of ongoing trauma and discrimination. It is not the responsibility of the community to educate you.

4.) **Never show up empty-handed**
Showing up in support is great but offer to lend a hand as well. Use your labour, resources and skills to help out. What additional value can you bring the community?

5.) **Always seek consent and permission**
Consent is a continuous process, not a one-time request. Seek permission before taking part in community events, particularly around cultural and spiritual events. They'll usually be labeled something like 'all community and allies welcome'.

6.) **Be responsible for yourself**
Be aware of what resources you're taking away from communities through your presence. Ensure you've given back to the community more than you've taken away.

7.) **Know when to step back**
Be aware of what space you are taking up. Always remember that you are there as a guest in a supportive role. There will be times when the community needs to act alone, respect their boundaries.

8.) **Saviours are not needed, solidarity is**
Solidarity is only meaningful if it is substantive and not merely performative. This means showing up to support the community with your presence alone should be the baseline, not the end game.

9.) **Be mindful of others' time and energy**
First Nations people often have to be advocates on a wide range of issues that affect them and their community first-hand. They don't have the choice to switch off from being involved and can be spread thin in many directions.

10.) **Do no harm to the community**
The community should be better off, or the same, because of your presence, not worse. Follow all of these suggestions and keep reflecting on your behaviour and you're on your way to doing your part in bringing down an unjust system.[2]

BECOME EDUCATED...
THEN EDUCATE!

*Education is what got us into this mess — the use of education at least in terms of Residential Schools — but **education is the key to reconciliation... We need to look at the way we are educating children.** That's why we say that this is not an Aboriginal problem. It's a Canadian problem.*

- *Murray Sinclair* [3]

As you become more educated on this dark chapter of our history you can begin to share that information with others. We recommend that you seek out educational materials on Residential Schools, Survivor stories and the process of reconciliation. Through your education, you will understand the importance of changing the education system in Canada so that Canada's traumatic history is not hidden. In order to create change, we must be equipped with the truths of the past.

When teachers and adults take initiatives to educate themselves on these topics, children become more aware of how they can be forces for positive change. As you become educated on the history of our past and the mistreatment of Indigenous peoples in Canada, you can make informed choices on how to create a new legacy and inspire reconciliation.

BE FLEXIBLE

Learning about Residential Schools, Survivor stories and reconciliation can be challenging because it involves the process of **unlearning** old ways of thinking. In the past, history books have not always included the facts and tragic details about Residential Schools and acts of cultural genocide.

Now, with the Orange Shirt Day movement and reconciliation, we have an opportunity to re-educate ourselves. Through this re-education, or re-learning, we can become fully aware of how the past impacts our future.

Being flexible means being willing to look at the past, present and future from a new perspective.

Unlearning is the process of discarding or overriding learned habits, lessons and concepts.

Orange Shirt Day at Glenlawn Collegiate school. Photo courtesy of Glenlawn Collegiate.

SCHOOLS

If you are a school or educational institution, there are many opportunities to support Indian Residential School reconciliation by participating in Orange Shirt Day activities. From Kindergarten to University, students rally on a yearly basis to raise awareness of the impacts of Residential Schools on Survivors, their families and their communities.

Here are some suggestions:

- Invite an Elder to your school to speak about Residential Schools and their impacts. Please ensure that you host the Elder with generosity, kindness and respect. Part of showing respect is following the traditional protocol of the area in which you reside. Please consult with local Indigenous communities or your Indigenous educational consultant to learn how to do that in a respectful way.
- Attend a public Orange Shirt Day event if there is one in your community
- Host your own Orange Shirt Day. This could include, but is not limited to, sharing Phyllis's story, reading her books and watching videos online.
- Decorating orange shirts to wear on September 30th

Orange Shirt Society speaker Phyllis Webstad is available, on a limited basis, to offer presentations to schools, universities and corporations across the country, both in-person and virtually. The Orange Shirt Society is working on developing a network of speakers and video presentations to create new educational opportunities.

A teacher's study guide has been created as a companion to the Orange Shirt Day textbook. After reading Orange Shirt Day and completing the end-of-chapter questions and activities, this study guide can then be used to expand your Orange Shirt Day education. It includes several concepts and ideas from within the book that have been expanded on and are intended to inspire you to dig deeper.

The Orange Shirt Day Study Guide can be purchased at *www.medicinewheelpublishing.com*.

CREATE ARTWORK

During the month of September, countless classrooms and students passionately create art that represents Orange Shirt Day and what they've learned about Indian Residential School Reconciliation.

Popular topics include:

• Using orange shirt cutouts and writing "Every Child Matters"
• Writing "Every Child Matters" on hearts and placing the hearts around the school
• Writing exercises on "what reconciliation means to you" and "How I am participating in Orange Shirt Day"
• Decorating orange shirts to wear on September 30th

Orange Shirt Day inspired artwork by grade 7 student Noor Bajwa.

Creating art is a positive and cathartic way to express how one is affected by an experience or subject. Using art to express how Residential Schools and reconciliation affects you can inspire the journey of others and provoke thoughtful conversation. As well, creating artwork is a form of personal reconciliation because it helps you to process knowledge, thoughts, emotions and life-events that affect you in any way.

In the fall of 2019, Medicine Wheel Education along with the Orange Shirt Society hosted an art contest that saw hundreds of kids from around Canada submit artwork and writing pieces that detailed what Orange Shirt Day and Residential School reconciliation means to them. Throughout this book you will see many of the incredible pieces submitted to us! While it was not possible to feature every piece received, the Orange Shirt Society saw every piece and thanks those who took the time to participate in this project and share their personal experiences.

ACKNOWLEDGE THE TRADITIONAL TERRITORY

Educate yourself as to the traditional territory on which you are situated. To show respect and as an act of reconciliation, ensure you acknowledge the traditional territory at the beginning of any gathering or assembly in the proper protocol of the territory.

GET TO KNOW INDIGENOUS RESOURCES

Explore the different Indigenous resources within your community. These resources may vary from youth mentorship programs, therapeutic services, cultural studies classes, local history books, plant medicine teachings or local calls to action. There is a wide variety of Indigenous resources available to you, and as the passion for Residential School reconciliation broadens more resources will be created.

Additionally, if you find you require crisis support, at any time, there are helpline numbers available in the introduction of this book.

TRUTH AND RECONCILIATION COMMISSION RESOURCES

The Truth and Reconciliation Commission of Canada (TRC) has created resources that can be used to effectively understand the truth of what took place in the Residential School System. Some resources included *They Came for the Children* (interim report), the TRC final report which gives 94 Calls To Action for change and a map of government-sponsored Residential Schools in Canada. The map can be found on page 26, at the start of Chapter 3. These are all excellent resources to further understand what took place in the Residential School System.

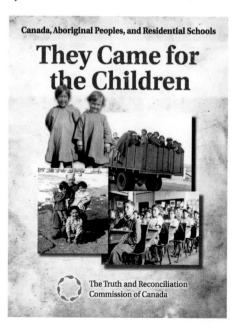

Brothers Christopher N. and David N. at an Orange Shirt Day event in Toronto 2019. Photo taken by Nadya Kwandibens of Red Works Photography.

BE THOUGHTFUL & BE EMPATHETIC

"

*The best way to acknowledge Truth and Reconciliation Day is to be present. Attend a community event and be present. **Listen to Survivors by opening your mind, your heart and your spirit. Make space for them as they share their stories. Be attentive while they speak. Bear witness to their story.***

*Please remember, the elderly grandparent that is speaking was only a child when they endured those horrors. **Be mindful that they still may be bitter, hurt and angry. That's okay.** Although it may feel uncomfortable to listen, it is a small gesture we can all do to help the Survivors on their journey of healing.*

***After they are done, give thanks. Give a smile, a nod or a hug.** Whatever you are comfortable with and deem appropriate. By doing so, you are acknowledging the strength, courage and resilience they have just displayed by sharing their truth.*

"

- Ren Louie [4]

Ren Louie speaks at Orange Shirt Day on Camosun's Lansdowne Campus, Victoria, B.C. on September 28, 2019. Photo courtesy of Camosun College AV.

ORANGE JERSEY PROJECT

The Orange Jersey Project was born out of an idea. 'What if we could use the power of sport to serve as a vehicle toward educating today's young athletes about the history of the Indian Residential School System and strengthen the path toward truth and reconciliation with Indigenous Peoples.'

The inspirational idea of the Orange Jersey Project was born from Tyler Fuller — an Indigenous man from Kawatoose First Nation in Saskatchewan. The idea was born from Fuller's experience watching the devastating news that came from Kamloops Indian Residential School, and the 215 unmarked graves that were found…. He reached out to his long time friend, Chief Willie Sellars from the Sugar Cane Band, located outside of Williams Lake BC who introduced Fuller to Phyllis Webstad, the creator and founder of the Orange Shirt Society. Fuller and Webstad discussed his idea.

Together, the Orange Shirt Society and the Orange Jersey Project have evolved into a nationally recognized organization making an impact. With assistance from Canadian Tire, Orange Shirt Society and the Orange Jersey Project have been fortunate to have minor hockey teams across Turtle Island participate and receive free jerseys. Teams wear orange practice jerseys as a way to educate themselves and others with the quote, "Why Orange?". The Orange Shirt Society and the Orange Jersey Project have also developed a Learning Module System for young Indigenous and non-Indigenous athletes to learn and educate themselves from coast-to-coast.

If you want to register your hockey team, visit the Orange Jersey Project at *orangejerseyproject.ca* and you can participate in the truth and reconciliation movement through sports. [5]

The Orange Jersey Project Logo was created, in part, by Shayne Hommy whose design was the Official Orange Shirt Day Design for 2021. At the time Shayne won, Shayne was a Grade 11 First Nation Cree student at South Peace Secondary School, in Dawson Creek. Her design means justice and awareness for Indigenous people.

BUSINESSES

Businesses are at the center of activities in the community. Whenever there are sensitive or heartbreaking announcements taking place, be aware and be sensitive. There are many ways in which a business can show up to support Indigenous communities during these difficult times. Here are several ways you can share these messages as a local business:

- Put posters or calls for action on your bulletin boards
- Stock local Indigenous history books and Phyllis Webstad's Orange Shirt Story books
- Display the Orange Shirt Day logo that says, "Every Child Matters"
- Allow your business to become an advocate for social change and Indigenous injustices in Canada

WRITE A LETTER

Write a letter to your local, provincial or national government encouraging greater efforts for reconciliation and awareness of Orange Shirt Day. As you educate yourself on your reconciliation resources, you may become aware of what actions need to take place to create change. By using your voice to call for action, you are actively participating in helping to establish an environment that supports healing, recovery and reconciliation.

Writing a letter is a participatory act that can be done at any time of the year, and ultimately supports the mission of Orange Shirt Day and the Orange Shirt Society.

DONATE

If you feel moved to donate to the Orange Shirt Society, you can do so through the website.

www.orangeshirtday.org

THE OFFICIAL ORANGE SHIRT DAY SHIRT

Every year the Orange Shirt Society chooses an official orange shirt design. You could be the one sharing your design. To learn more please visit www.orangeshirtday.org.

The official shirt of 2023 was created by Charliss Santos, a grade 10 student.

"For me, Orange Shirt Day is a day of reminiscence, where we look back on our dark past and reflect on the actions we have given to the First Nation's People. My design showcases an Indigenous child between two hands, people, a heart and an eagle... **The child symbolises all Indigenous children who have suffered inside Residential Schools.** *The people represent the strong community the First Nation's people have built…* **The heart represents healing and forgiveness, and lastly, the eagle represents acceptance, honesty and freedom.** *I wear my orange shirt to show my support for the Indigenous community, and to tell them that they are not alone in their healing process."*

- Charliss Santos, Grade 10 Student [6]

CHAPTER FIVE QUESTIONS
REFLECTION ON LEARNING

1. What does Orange Shirt Day have the power to do?

2. Are there any limits on how you can participate in Orange Shirt day?

3. What should you consider when purchasing a shirt for Orange Shirt Day?

4. Are you welcome to create your own Orange Shirt? If so, what does it need to include?

5. Regardless of where you get your shirt, what message should be on the shirt and what colour should it be?

6. What are some of the books available to learn about Phyllis's story?

7. Why is it important to become an ally, supporting Indigenous Peoples? How can you become an advocate for Orange Shirt Day?

8. What are some of the things that are important for allies to remember according to Amnesty International? Why is it important to remember these things?

9. Murray Sinclair said "education is the key to reconciliation". What do you think he means when he says this? How can education be a key to this process?

10. What are some of the ways that schools can participate?

11. Why is creating art a positive way of expressing how learning about Residential Schools and reconciliation affects you?

12. What are some ways that people can be a part of the movement?

13. In what ways can we be thoughtful and empathetic toward events focused on healing and reconciliation?

14. How did Tyler Fuller honour the history of the Indian Residential School System?

15. What do the symbols on the official Orange Shirt for 2023 represent?

16. What does "holding a space for Survivors and their families to share their experiences" mean? Why is this important in regards to the goals of Orange Shirt Day?

17. Your participation and education will also help you to confront racism, stereotypes and prejudices against Indigenous people. In order to be effective at confronting racism, stereotypes and prejudices, what do you think that education needs to include?

18. What are territory acknowledgements and how do they relate to walking a path of reconciliation?

RESEARCH

1. Getting to know Indigenous resources in your community is critical to increasing your education. What are some Indigenous resources available to you and your school? You can create a list, a PowerPoint presentation, or a poster.

2. Research what should be included in a territorial acknowledgement. Using this information, write one for the territory on which you are currently living.

ACTIVITY

Create an informational poster with resources:

Use your creativity to make it visually appealing!

Create a Poem using the word O.R.A.N.G.E.

Have each letter represent a word or sentence relating to Orange Shirt Day.

O _____

R _____

A _____

N _____

G _____

E _____

SOURCES

1. "10 WAYS TO BE A GENUINE ALLY TO FIRST NATIONS COMMUNITIES"
    <https://www.amnesty.org.au/10-ways-to-be-an-ally-to-first-nations-communities/> accessed February 1st, 2023.
2. "10 WAYS TO BE A GENUINE ALLY TO FIRST NATIONS COMMUNITIES"
    <https://www.amnesty.org.au/10-ways-to-be-an-ally-to-first-nations-communities/> accessed February 1st, 2023.
3. "Truth and Reconciliation Chair Urges Canada to Adopt UN Declaration on Indigenous Peoples." CBC News. Haydn Watters. June 1, 2015.
    <https://www.cbc.ca/1.3096225?__vfz=medium%3Dsharebar> accessed May 15, 2020.
4. Louie, Ren. Personal Interview. February, 2023.
5. "Orange Jersey Project." <https://orangejerseyproject.ca/> accessed January, 2023.
6. Santos, Charliss. Official Orange Shirt Shirt Design Art Submission. March, 2023.

Medicine hearts filled with traditional medicines including tobacco, cedar, sweet grass and sage. Photo courtesy of Jacqueline Maurer and the Dze L K'ant Friendship Centre on the Wet'suwet'en Territory.

CHAPTER 6 RECONCILIATION
BUILDING A FUTURE TOGETHER

The Orange Shirt Society is always exploring and striving to have a greater understanding of reconciliation and what it means for Canadians. The Society's first purpose is "to support Indian Residential School Reconciliation."

During the course of researching and interviewing people for this book, it became apparent that there are many views of reconciliation and that they are all valid. A person's view of reconciliation will depend on their experiences, cultural heritage, upbringing, education, and where they live. When combined, this makes up their worldview.

Oxford dictionary defines worldview as:
"A largely unconscious but generally coherent set of presuppositions and beliefs that every person has which shape how we make sense of the world and everything in it. This in turn influences such things as how we see ourselves as individuals, how we interpret our role in society, how we deal with social issues, and what we regard as truth." [1]

The Orange Shirt Society decided to present some of those views and challenge you, the reader, to figure out what reconciliation means to you. As you walk your personal journey of reconciliation the Society also challenges you to participate in discussions and think about how it affects your classmates, school, families and communities.

There is no right and wrong way to explore reconciliation.

In 2014, the Assembly of First Nation's Chiefs in Council passed a resolution supporting Orange Shirt Day stating "Call upon all Canadians to listen with open hearts to the stories of survivors and those affected by Residential School to fully comprehend each other. This is a first step in reconciliation." [2]

In this chapter, the Society has heavily quoted from the Truth and Reconciliation Commission's (TRC) final report issued in June, 2015, which is available in its entirety at www.trc.ca. The final report ends with 94 Calls to Action stating, "in order to redress the legacy of Residential Schools and advance the process of Canadian reconciliation…". [3] They are directed at governments, schools, businesses, and all Canadians, and they call on all of us to implement change.

Children marching for Orange Shirt Day in Shulus, B.C. Photo taken by Dara Hill of the Merritt Herald.

Artwork by Fern Hill School student Sabriyya Ashe

WHAT ARE PEOPLE SAYING ABOUT RECONCILIATION?

There are many facets of reconciliation in Canada that people are engaged in. The Orange Shirt Society focuses on Indian Residential School Reconciliation which also includes the process and the personal journey. In this context, reconciliation is new and people are still trying to understand and trust it.

Reconciliation in the Oxford English Dictionary is defined as:

"an end to a disagreement or conflict with somebody and the start of a good relationship…". [4]

Anne Burrill, one of the founders of Orange Shirt Day, said, *"reconciliation is both a personal journey and a public process."* [5]

The Truth and Reconciliation Commission described reconciliation as *"an ongoing individual and collective process, and will require commitment from all those affected including First Nations, Inuit and Métis former Indian Residential School students, their families, communities, religious entities, former school employees, government and the people of Canada. Reconciliation may occur between any of the above groups."* [6]

The Truth and Reconciliation Commission stated, *"reconciliation is about establishing... a respectful relationship between Aboriginal and non-Aboriginal peoples in this country. For that to happen, there has to be awareness of the past, acknowledgement of the harm that has been inflicted, atonement for the causes, and action to change behaviour".* [7]

Elder Stephen Augustine said, *"...there is both a place for talking about reconciliation and a need for quiet reflection. Reconciliation cannot occur without listening, contemplation, meditation, and deeper internal deliberation."* [8]

British Columbia Premier John Horgan said, *"Reconciliation is hard work. It does not begin or end with a single decision, event or moment. No single one of us decides what reconciliation can or should look like. It is a shared journey we are on together. We know that this work isn't easy. If we're going to achieve it, we have to stay committed to this process, keep engaging with one another and find common ground."* [9]

As a founding member of the Reconciliation Canada initiative and a generous supporter of the Orange Shirt Society, Vancity states that:

"The reconciliation process is important for all Canadians because it's about the basics of how we treat each other as fellow human beings and the kind of relationships and communities we want to build for the future...

For many Canadians we don't really know much about the ongoing impact of Indian Residential Schools—how it continues to be felt throughout generations and contribute to social problems… More than 150,000 First Nations, Métis, and Inuit children were placed in these schools. Connections with culture and family, parenting skills, and intergenerational relationships were damaged or lost. People were broken. It's time to acknowledge and understand the past, and find a new way forward." [10]

Lorena Fontaine, a participant in an Aboriginal Women's digital storytelling project on intergenerational reconciliation, said, *"reconciliation is about stories and our ability to tell stories. I think the intellectual part of ourselves wants to start looking for words to define reconciliation. And then there is the heart knowledge that comes from our life experiences. It's challenging to connect the two and relate it to reconciliation..."* [11]

Chief Fred Robbins says, *"the monuments [that were erected in the SJM commemoration] were intended for people, to reconcile the spirits of Residential School Survivors and provide freedom to be themselves as triumphant First Nations people. During the reunion, I felt First Nations being heard by mainstream society for the first time in Williams Lake. For the first time, non-First Nations people were aware of the Residential School. In general, reconciliation is recognizing that something happened, that healing needs to happen, otherwise it can still happen."* [12]

Chief Fred Robbins with one of two commemorative monuments. Photo by Monica Lamb-Yorski of the Williams Lake Tribune.

THE RECONCILIATION PROCESS

Through the making of this book, there were three themes that were undeniably evident as prerequisites for reconciliation in Canada. These three themes are education, truth telling, and recognizing our shared history.

EDUCATION

The cornerstone of reconciliation is education. Many Indigenous leaders, including Murray Sinclair, Chief Fred Robbins and Phyllis Webstad, have discussed the critical importance of education moving forward with reconciliation in Canada.

Senator and TRC chair Murray Sinclair stated that *"seven Generations of children went through the Residential Schools. Each of those children who were educated were told that their lives were not as good as the non-Aboriginal people of this country. They were told that their languages and their culture were irrelevant...* **As a result, many generations of children, including you and your parents, have been raised to think about things in a different way... in a way that is negative when it comes to Aboriginal people. We need to change that. It is the educational system that has contributed to this problem in this country and it is the educational system that, we believe, will help us get away from this. We need to look at the way we educate children. We need to look at the way we educate ourselves. We need to look at what our textbooks say about Aboriginal people. We need to look at what it is Aboriginal people themselves are allowed to say within the educational systems about their own histories...** *Because it took us so many generations to get to this point it's going to take us at least a few generations to say that we are making progress. We cannot look for quick and easy solutions, because there are none. We need to be able to look at this from the perspective of where do we want to be in three, four, five or seven generations from now when we talk about the relationship between Aboriginal and non-Aboriginal people in this country. If we can agree on what that relationship needs to look like in the future, then what we need to think about is what can we do today that will contribute to that objective. Reconciliation will be about ensuring that everything we are doing today is aimed at that high standard of restoring that balance to that relationship."* [13]

Senator Murray Sinclair, as the Chief Commissioner for the Truth and Reconciliation Commission, said, *"…as a commission we have said we have to start addressing the way we teach our children about Aboriginal people. We have to address how we teach our children about Canadian history so that they can grow up understanding that things are not as rosy as some schools have been teaching them. We have to teach them properly about the invalidity of the **doctrine of discovery**."* [14]

Chief Fred Robbins' story offers perspective of lack of education around the existence of Residential Schools.

"I rode with a prominent member of the School District to a soccer tournament once, and they asked about my childhood. To my surprise they had no clue that there was a Residential School here. Also Kerry Cook (former mayor of Williams Lake) told me that her knowledge of the Residential School was the pool she used to swim in. We weren't allowed to swim in it. And, when I revisited the 150 Mile Elementary School (where I attended class when I lived at the Residential School), where my old classmate was now principal, he didn't know that I went 'home' each night to the horrors of the Residential School." [15]

The TRC Final Report states that, *"…all students – Aboriginal and non-Aboriginal – need to learn that the history of this country did not begin with the arrival of Jacques Cartier on the banks of the St. Lawrence River. They need to learn about the Indigenous Nations the Europeans met, about their rich linguistic and cultural heritage, …"* [16]

TRUTH TELLING

In order to achieve reconciliation every person must make the effort to listen to the painful truths of what took place in Residential Schools as well as the intergenerational impacts. Orange Shirt Day opens the door to conversations of all aspects of Residential School and provides a safe place for Survivors and their families to tell their truths.

Phyllis Webstad says that *"the truth of what happened needs to be told and understood in order for Reconciliation to happen. I, as a Survivor, call upon all Canadians to open their minds and hearts to hear our truths."* [17]

Kerry Cook, the mayor of Williams Lake during the time of the commemoration project events, reflected on her relationship with Chief Fred Robbins. She said, *"I remember his courage for speaking his truth. His strength and vulnerability came from somewhere deep inside of him and as he shared his story it stirred or awakened something deep inside of me. It is not very often that you experience a divine encounter; a shared vision that awakens your very soul. Looking back it was as though the soil of my heart had been prepared for this very moment. When he shared his vision it was as though he was planting a seed deep into my heart."* [18]

OUR SHARED HISTORY

The painful history of Indian Residential Schools belongs to all Canadians. Now it is every Canadian's responsibility to learn about the past and make informed choices in the present moment that create an inclusive future.

Phyllis Webstad stated *"this isn't just Indigenous history, this is Canadian history."* [19]

Murray Sinclair declares that *"reconciliation overall, from the commission's perspective, means that we also have to convince Canadian society that this is their story as well."* [20]

The Truth and Reconciliation Commission's final report shares one non-Indigenous woman's experience. She said, *"by listening to your story, my story can change. By listening to your story, I can change."* [21]

RECONCILIATION IS THE FUTURE

The movement of Orange Shirt Day has shown us that people, especially Canada's youth, are committed to creating a bright future in which reconciliation is a way of life.

Chief Fred Robbins feels that, *"reconciliation must happen in due course. You can't put a timeline on it. Once reconciliation is accomplished at some level, there needs to be restitution, giving us back our authority, it has to be different."* [22]

Phyllis Webstad passionately states that her objective is *"to keep telling my story so that people in the world will know first hand what has gone on and that it will never be repeated. For my grandchildren, that they will live different and better lives and the lives of future generations will increasingly improve in this new world we create. We are all here, no one is going away. We need to learn to live together, and to respect each other."* [23]

Elder Barney Williams, member of the Truth and Reconciliation Commission's Survivor Committee, said, *"I think more and more people are realizing that the engagement of youth is crucial. For me, as a Survivor, I'm really impressed with how much they knew. I was very impressed with the type of questions the audience asked. It tells me, as somebody who's carried this pain for over sixty-eight years, that there's hope. Finally there's hope on the horizon and it's coming from the right place. It's coming from the youth."* [24]

Murray Sinclair declared, *"I really don't care if you feel responsible for the past. The real question is do you feel a sense of responsibility for the future because that's what this is all about."* [25]

Phyllis said, *"I read recently that reconciliation is dead. When I read that I thought no it isn't! The seed of reconciliation is being planted in elementary and high schools across Canada".* [26]

When discussing the future, Murray Sinclair said,
"…reconciliation isn't going to come easily, it took us 150 years of these schools to create this damage. You know, my grandfather was a carpenter and he used to tell me, 'It's a lot easier to knock something down than it is to build it.' They [the Canadian Government] spent 150 years knocking things down, so it may take us that long to build it back up again. But, we have to build it up…We have to learn how to get along and we have to learn how to get along respectfully." [27]

"Our future, and the well-being of all our children rests with the kind of relationships we build today" says Chief Dr. Robert Joseph. O.B.C. a Residential School Survivor and founder of Reconciliation Canada. [28]

The artwork that children created using Orange Shirt Day and reconciliation as their inspiration shows us that Phyllis and Elder Barney Williams are correct. Canada's youth are more passionate than ever about restoring Indigenous rights and revealing their collective truths. Murray Sinclair reminds us that reconciliation is going to take time to rebuild and move forward together. The process requires all of us to walk on the journey towards understanding reconciliation.

RECONCILIATION AND THE PATH FORWARD

Whatever your path to reconciliation looks like, keep forging ahead. The journey may not be easy at times, but your contributions are guaranteed to change the future. Remember that you are not on this journey alone. Phyllis Webstad, the Orange Shirt Society and many other people are walking this path with you. Actions taken and commitments made today will affect future generations of Canadians.

The Truth and Reconciliation Commission final report states that, *"All Canadians must make a firm and lasting commitment to reconciliation in order to ensure that Canada is a country where our children and grandchildren can thrive."* [29]

When asked if he had any advice for non-Indigenous Canadians, Chief Fred Robbins had this to say: *"Spread the word. Stay the path. Know that you're not just helping yourself to learn and understand, you're helping generations of Residential School Survivors. The term "ally", comrade-in-arms, means that you understand although you haven't lived it so you can't fully, and you want to make it better. When speaking from the heart, there is no way to lose if coming from the heart, no right or wrong."* [30]

At Queen's University, in their Faculty of Law building, there is a powerful Murray Sinclair quote that reads, *"the road we travel is equal in importance to the destination we seek. There are no shortcuts. When it comes to truth and reconciliation we are forced to go the distance."* [31]

Phyllis Webstad signs a student made blanket at Chester Area Middle School on January 27, 2020 in Nova Scotia. Photo by Sarah Philbrick.

The last word is from Phyllis Webstad:

*"During my time presenting to schools and organizations across Canada, I met some astounding and amazing people of all ages and races. **What I witnessed first-hand is that people care**, that they want to hear our truths, and that they are committed to the process of reconciliation. When people know better, they can do better. When I get a chance to speak to Survivors directly, I'm always sure to tell them about this and how I believe that our future is in good hands. **One day there will be no survivors left in Canada, and I want other Survivors to know we can leave this earth knowing that the children are learning about what happened to us and they empathize, and they will make sure it never happens again.**"* [32]

CHAPTER SIX QUESTIONS
REFLECTION ON LEARNING

1. Why are there "many views of reconciliation"? To what extent is the statement "there is no right and wrong way to explore reconciliation" true? Are there ways that may not be appropriate? If so, in what ways?
2. What makes up one's worldview?
3. In your own words, explain the Oxford dictionary definition of reconciliation?
4. If the "first step to reconciliation" is to "call upon all Canadians to listen with open hearts to the stories of Survivors and those affected by Residential School to fully comprehend each other," what might be the next steps that people might take on this journey?
5. Fill in the blanks. Anne Burrill stated "reconciliation is both a _____ journey and a _____ process." What might she mean?
6. Fill in the blanks. The Truth and Reconciliation Commission states that reconciliation is "an _____ individual and collective _____, and will require _____ from all those affected including First Nations, Inuit and Métis former Indian Residential School students, their families, communities, religious entities, former school employees, government and the people of Canada. _____ may occur between any of the above groups." In what ways does it require commitment? Why?
7. Fill in the blanks. BC Premiere John Horgan stated "reconciliation is _____ work. It does not begin or end with a _____ decision, event or moment. No single one of us decides what reconciliation can or should look like. It is a _____ journey." What does he mean by this statement?
8. Fill in the blanks. Chief Fred Robbins says, "the monuments [that were erected in the SJM commemoration] were intended for _____, to reconcile the _____ of Residential School Survivors and provide _____ to be themselves as _____First Nations people. During the reunion, I felt First Nations being _____by mainstream society for the first time in Williams Lake. For the first time, non-First Nations people were _____ of the Residential School. In general, reconciliation is_____ that something happened, that _____ needs to happen, otherwise it can still _____." Why do you think it could otherwise still happen?
9. Fill in the blanks. Vancity states that "the reconciliation process is important for all _____because it's about the basics of how we _____ each other as fellow _____ and the kind of _____ and _____ we want to build for the _____... For many Canadians we don't really know much about the ongoing _____ of Indian Residential Schools—how it _____ to be felt throughout _____and contribute to _____... More than _____ First Nations, Métis, and Inuit children were placed in these schools. _____with culture and family, _____skills, and _____ relationships were _____ or lost. People were _____. It's time to _____ and _____ the past, and a new way _____."
10. What are the three themes that were evident as required for reconciliation in Canada? In what ways is each important in recognizing our shared history? What do others say about each of these three themes?
11. What stands out for you in the statements made about how reconciliation is the future? Why do you think these stand out for you?
12. Fill in the blanks. The Truth and Reconciliation Commission final report states that, "All Canadians must make a _____ and_____ commitment to_____ in order to ensure that _____is a country where our children and grandchildren can_____."
13. Fill in the blanks. Chief Fred Robbins provided the following advice: "Spread the _____. Stay the _____. Know that you're not just _____ yourself to _____ and _____, you're helping _____ of Residential School Survivors. The term _____, comrade-in-arms, means that you _____ although you haven't_____ it so you can't fully, and you want to make it _____. When speaking from the_____, there is no way to_____ if coming from the heart, no_____ or _____."What does this mean to you?
14. Fill in the blanks. Murray Sinclair stated "the _____ we travel is equal in _____ to the _____ we seek. There are no _____. When it comes to _____ and ____·_____ we are forced to go the _____."What might he mean?
15. What did Phyllis Webstad witness in her time presenting to schools and organizations? Why does she believe that the future of Survivors and their families is in good hands?
16. What does Reconciliation mean to you? What are some actions that you are able to take to participate in the process?
17. Residential Schools were in operation for over one hundred years and impacts are still felt today. What do you think Reconciliation will look like in the next one hundred years? How will the lives of Indigenous people be different?
18. Find an example of someone in this book or beyond that demonstrated walking the path to reconciliation. What did they do? What inspired them? What impact did they have?

RESEARCH

Now that you have learned a lot about reconciliation and Orange Shirt Day, imagine you are in charge of hosting an Orange Shirt Day event.
Write up a day plan with details about your event including the following:
• What will people do?
• How will you advertise the event?
• How will you engage people in conversations about Residential Schools?
• Who would you invite to the event?
• How do you host an Elder at your event with respect and generosity?
Refer to www.orangeshirtday.org for more resources and ideas.

SOURCES

1. "Worldview." Oxford Reference. <https://www.oxfordreference.com/view/10.1093/oi/authority.20110803124830471> accessed May 15, 2020.

2. "Assembly of First Nations 2014 General Assembly, Halifax, N.S." <https://www.afn.ca/uploads/files/afn_aga_2014_resolutions_final_en.pdf> accessed May 25, 2020. pp. 18.

3. "Truth and Reconciliation Commission of Canada: Calls to Action." Truth and Reconciliation Commission of Canada. 2015.<http://trc.ca/assets/pdf/Calls_to_Action_English2.pdf> accessed February 1, 2020.

4. "Reconciliation." Oxford Learner's Dictionaries. <https://www.oxfordlearnersdictionaries.com/definition/english/reconciliation> accessed May 25, 2020.

5. "Artist Workshops to Focus on Reconciliation." The Williams Lake Tribune. <https://www.wltribune.com/community/artist-workshops-to-focus-on-reconciliation/> accessed May 24, 2020

6. "Our Mandate." Truth and Reconciliation Commission of Canada. <http://www.trc.ca/about-us/our-mandate.html> accessed April 20, 2020.

7. "Canada's Residential Schools: Reconciliation. The Final Report of the Truth and Reconciliation Commission of Canada. Volume 6." Truth and Reconciliation Commission of Canada. McGill-Queen's University Press, Montreal & Kingston, London, Chicago. 2015. <http://www.trc.ca/assets/pdf/Volume_6_Reconciliation_English_Web.pdf> accessed May 24, 2020. pp. 3.

8. "Honoring the Truth, Reconciling for the Future. Summary of the Final Report of Truth and Reconciliation Commission of Canada." Truth and Reconciliation Commission of Canada. 2015. <http://www.trc.ca/assets/pdf/Honouring_the_Truth_Reconciling_for_the_Future_July_23_2015.pdf> accessed pp. 17.

9. "Victoria Police Investigating Reports of Assault at Wet'suwet'en Protect at BC Legislature." Chek News. Julian Kolsut and Tess Straaten. Vancouver. Febuary 11, 2020. <https://www.cheknews.ca/protests-continue-in-victoria-ahead-of-throne-speech-645602/> accessed May 24, 2020.

10. "Reconciliation Canada." Vancity. <https://www.vancity.com/AboutVancity/InvestingInCommunities/Partnerships/ReconciliationCanada/> accessed May 24, 2020.

11. "Honouring the Truth, Reconciling for the Future. Summary of the Final Report of Truth and Reconciliation Commission of Canada." Truth and Reconciliation Commission of Canada. 2015. <http://www.trc.ca/assets/pdf/Honouring_the_Truth_Reconciling_for_the_Future_July_23_2015.pdf> accessed on May 20, 2020. pp. 242.

12. Robbins, Chief Fred. Personal Interview. February. 2020.

13. "Justice and Federal Commissioner Murray Sinclair Speech." Truth and Reconciliation Commission. The Commemoration Project Events. Filmed by John Dell. Signal Point Media, 2013. DVD.

14. "Justice and Federal Commissioner Murray Sinclair Speech." Truth and Reconciliation Commission. The Commemoration Project Events. Filmed by John Dell. Signal Point Media, 2013. DVD.

15. Robbins, Chief Fred. Personal Interview. February. 2020.

16. "Canada's Residential Schools: Reconciliation. The Final Report of the Truth and Reconciliation Commission of Canada. Volume 6." Truth and Reconciliation Commission of Canada. 2015. McGill-Queen's University Press, Montreal & Kingston, London, Chicago. <http://www.trc.ca/assets/pdf/Volume_6_Reconciliation_English_Web.pdf> accessed May 24, 2020. pp. 119.

17. Webstad, Phyllis. Personal Interview. January. 2020

18. Cook, Kerry. Personal Interview. March. 2020.

19. Webstad, Phyllis. Personal Interview. January. 2020.

20. "Justice and Federal Commissioner Murray Sinclair Speech." Truth and Reconciliation Commission. The Commemoration Project Events. Filmed by John Dell. Signal Point Media, 2013. DVD.

21. "Final Report of the Truth and Reconciliation Commission of Canada, Volume 1." Truth and Reconciliation Canada. <http://www.trc.ca/assets/pdf/Volume_1_History_Part_1_English_Web.pdf> accessed May 2, 2020. pp. 21.

22. Robbins, Chief Fred. Personal Interview. Febuary. 2020.

23. Webstad, Phyllis. Personal Interview. January. 2020.

24. "Honouring the Truth, Reconciling for the Future. Summary of the Final Report of Truth and Reconciliation Commission of Canada." Truth and Reconciliation Commission of Canada. 2015. <http://www.trc.ca/assets/pdf/Honouring_the_Truth_Reconciling_for_the_Future_July_23_2015.pdf> accessed on May 20, 2020. pp. 243.

25. "Justice and Federal Commissioner Murray Sinclair Speech." Truth and Reconciliation Commission. The Commemoration Project Events. Filmed by John Dell. Signal Point Media, 2013. DVD.

26. Webstad, Phyllis. Personal Interview. January. 2020.

27. "Justice and Federal Commissioner Murray Sinclair Speech. "Truth and Reconciliation Commission. The Commemoration Project Events. Filmed by John Dell. Signal Point Media, 2013. DVD.

28. "Reconciliation Canada." <https://reconciliationcanada.ca/> accessed on May 25, 2020.

29. "Honouring the Truth, Reconciling for the Future. Summary of the Final Report of Truth and Reconciliation Commission of Canada." Truth and Reconciliation Commission of Canada. 2015. <http://www.trc.ca/assets/pdf/Honouring_the_Truth_Reconciling_for_the_Future_July_23_2015.pdf> accessed on May 20, 2020. pp. 317.

30. Robbins, Chief Fred. Personal Interview. Febuary. 2020.

31. "Keeping reconciliation at the forefront." Queen's Gazette. September 12, 2019. <https://www.queensu.ca/gazette/stories/keeping-reconciliation-forefront> accessed May 25, 2020.

32. Webstad, Phyllis. Personal Interview. January. 2020.

Phyllis Webstad admiring student artwork at Desert Sands Community School, Ashcroft, B.C. presentation in 2019.

7 GLOSSARY

Allyship or being an ally is the process of building long-lasting relationships based on trust and respect.

Assimilation is the process of a minority cultural group being absorbed into a more dominant society resulting in the loss of culture, language, and knowledge.

A **band**, "or 'Indian Band', is a governing unit of Indians in Canada instituted by the Indian Act, 1876. The Indian Act defines a 'band' as a 'body of Indians.'" [1]

Children who didn't come home from Residential Schools because they died, from malnutrition, disease or injuries due to the circumstances and abuses endured at the schools. Many children also attempted to run away from the Residential Schools, but they died trying to find their way home. Records show that 6000 children died in Residential Schools, but the records are incomplete and it is believed that far more children didn't come home. There are ongoing investigations pertaining to the finding of unmarked and undocumented graves and burial sites at Residential School sites across Canada.[2]

Colonization occurs when settlers attempt to take over a foreign land by forcefully imposing their own politics and culture.

Doctrine of Discovery is the ideology that North America was "discovered" by Europeans. "The Doctrine of Discovery was used by European monarchies, beginning in the mid-fifteenth century, as a means of legitimizing the colonization of lands outside of Europe" by considering the land vacant or uninhabited. Even though Indigenous people were already living on these lands they were considered by Europeans to be non-human, thus justifying the "discovery." [3]

(Chief) **Fred Robbins** is Northern Secwépemc (Shuswap) from Esk'etemc First Nation (Alkali Lake). Chief Fred Robbins has a vision for reconciliation which involved all people remembering and learning what happened at St. Joseph's Mission Residential School, honouring and helping the Survivors recover from their experience and ultimately reconciling together.

First Nations "is a term used to describe Aboriginal peoples of Canada who are ethnically neither Métis nor Inuit." [4]

Genocide "means any of the following acts committed with intent to destroy, in whole or in part, a national, ethnical, racial or religious group, as such: Killing members of the group; Causing serious bodily or mental harm to members of the group; Deliberately inflicting on the group conditions of life calculated to bring about its physical destruction in whole or in part; Imposing measures intended to prevent births within the group; Forcibly transferring children of the group to another group." [5]

Indian is an erroneous and outdated term used to describe Indigenous People. It is based on the mistaken assumption by early European explorers that they had arrived in India. Unfortunately, it is still a 'legal' term employed within the 1876 Indian Act, which is still in use. Today 'Indian' is a derogatory term, and it will only be used in this book when referring to Indian Residential Schools and other legal terms within the Indian Act. [6]

The **Indian Act** is a Canadian federal law enacted in 1876 that allowed the government the regimented management of Indigenous peoples and their lands. The purpose of the Indian Act was to control, marginalize and oppress Indigenous people. [7]

An **Indian agent** was an administrator or representative for the Canadian government who had authority over Indigenous people and reserve lands. [8] As Phyllis Webstad explained "The Indian Agent had more power than the Chiefs and the Matriarchs." [9]

Indian Residential Schools (also referred to as Industrial schools)
"Residential Schools for Aboriginal people in Canada date back to the 1870s. Over 130 Residential Schools were located across the country, and the last school closed in 1996. These government-funded, church-run schools were set up to eliminate parental involvement in the intellectual, cultural, and spiritual development of Aboriginal children. During this era, more than 150,000 First Nations, Métis, and Inuit children were placed in these schools often against their parents' wishes. Many were forbidden to speak their language and practice their own culture. While there is an estimated 80,000 former students living today, the ongoing impact of Residential Schools has been felt throughout generations and has contributed to social problems that continue to exist." [10] The TRC only referred to Canadian government run schools. There were other Residential Schools and Day Schools across the country as early as 1620, run by churches and other organizations. [11]

Indian Residential School Reconciliation is an on going collective process that involves both Indigenous and non-Indigenous Canadians bravely acknowledging, and educating each other, on the mistreatment of Indigenous peoples through the Residential School system. Reconciliation aims to create a new legacy for Indigenous Canadians that supports a healing journey and sees a respectful resurgence of cultural traditions.

Indigenous, or, **Aboriginal**, people, "are the descendants of the original inhabitants of North America. The Canadian Constitution recognizes three groups of Aboriginal people - Indians, Métis and Inuit. These are three separate peoples with unique heritages, languages, cultural practices and spiritual beliefs." [12]

Intergenerational Survivor "refers to an individual who has been affected by the intergenerational dysfunction created by the experience of attending Residential School." [13]

Intergenerational Trauma is the transmission of historical oppression and its negative consequences across generations. [14]

John A MacDonald "As both prime minister and minister of Indian Affairs, Macdonald was responsible for Indigenous policy, including the development of the Residential School system and increasingly repressive measures against Indigenous populations." [15]

Inuit "Aboriginal people in Northern Canada, who live in Nunavut, Northwest Territories, Northern Quebec and Northern Labrador. The word means 'people' in the Inuit language —Inuktitut. The singular of Inuit is Inuk." [16]

Métis "means a person who self-identifies as Métis, is distinct from other Aboriginal peoples, is of historic Métis Nation Ancestry and who is accepted by the Métis Nation." [17]

National Day for Truth and Reconciliation "Each year, September 30 marks the National Day for Truth and Reconciliation. The day honours the children who never returned home and Survivors of Residential Schools, as well as their families and communities. Public commemoration of the tragic and painful history and ongoing impacts of residential schools is a vital component of the reconciliation process." [18] The day is considered a national federal statutory holiday.

A **national trauma** occurs when a traumatic event or experience effects a collective group of people across a country. Indian Residential Schools have resulted in a national trauma.

Orange Shirt Day occurs annually on September 30 and honours the Indigenous children who attended Indian Residential Schools, their families and the children who didn't come home. Orange Shirt Day encourages the education and awareness of Indian Residential School Reconciliation and proudly declares that 'Every Child Matters.'

The **Orange Shirt Society** is a non-profit organization, whose purposes are to promote Indian Residential School reconciliation, to raise awareness of the impacts of Indian Residential Schools, and their continuing intergenerational impacts, and to promote the concept of "Every Child Matters."

Phyllis Jack Webstad is a Residential School Survivor from the Stswecem'c Xget'tem (Canoe Creek/Dog Creek) First Nation in British Columbia. In 2013, Phyllis inspired the Orange Shirt Day movement by sharing the story of losing her shiny orange shirt on her first day of school at the St. Joseph Mission Residential School.

Racism is the discrimination against someone who is of a different race based on the belief that one race is superior to another.

Reconciliation - See Chapter 6

Reserves "An area of land set aside by the federal government for the use and occupancy of a First Nations group or band." [19]

Resilience is having the ability to sustain and recover from trauma and challenges.

St. Joseph's Mission Residential School was located just outside of Williams Lake, B.C. It opened in 1872 and closed in 1981. St. Joseph's Mission Residential School has also been called The Mission, Williams Lake Indian School, Williams Lake Industrial School, Cariboo Residential Industrial School and Cariboo Student Residence. [20]

Survivors are Indigenous people who attended Residential Schools and survived the experience, as some did not. The TRC estimated that as many as 6000 children died in the Residential Schools or as a result of the schools. [21]

The Truth and Reconciliation Commission (TRC) of Canada was founded on June 2nd, 2008 and aimed to reveal truths of Residential Schools and provide support for Survivor and their families. The TRC was created out of the Indian Residential School Settlement Agreement (IRSSA). [22]

Unlearning is the process of discarding or overriding learned habits, lessons and concepts.

The City of **Williams Lake** lies within the Cariboo Regional District of British Columbia and is situated on the traditional territory of the T'exelcemc (Williams Lake First Nation), members of the Secwépemc Nation (Shuswap People). [23]

Worldview: A largely unconscious but generally coherent set of presuppositions and beliefs that every person has which shape how we make sense of the world and everything in it. This in turn influences such things as how we see ourselves as individuals, how we interpret our role in society, how we deal with social issues, and what we regard as truth. [24]

SOURCES

1. "Bands." Indigenous Foundations UBC Arts. <https://indigenousfoundations.arts.ubc.ca/bands/> accessed May 25, 2020.
2. "Truth and Reconciliation Commission: By the Numbers." CBC News. Daniel Schwartz. June 3, 2015. <https://www.cbc.ca/news/indigenous/truth-and-reconciliation-commission-by-the-numbers-1.3096185> accessed May 1, 2020.

   "Truth and Reconciliation Commission: By the numbers." CBC News. Daniel Schwartz. June 3, 2015. <https://www.cbc.ca/news/indigenous/truth-and-reconciliation-commission-by-the-numbers-1.3096185> accessed May 1, 2020.

   "Residential Schools Findings Point to 'Cultural Genocide,' commission chair says." CBC News. John Paul Tasker. May 15, 2015. <https://www.cbc.ca/news/politics/residential-schools-ndings-point-to-cultural-genocide-commission-chair-says-1.3093580> accessed March 30, 2020.

   "Residential Schools Findings Point to 'Cultural Genocide,' Commission Chair Says." CBC News. John Paul Tasker. May 15, 2015. <https://www.cbc.ca/news/politics/residential-schools-findings-point-to-cultural-genocide-commission-chair-says-1.3093580> accessed March 30, 2020.
3. "Christopher Columbus and the Doctrine of Discovery: 5 Things to Know." Indigenous Corporate Training. October 3, 2016. <https://www.ictinc.ca/blog/christopher-columbus-and-the-doctrine-of-discovery-5-things-to-know> accessed by May 25, 2020.
4. "Terminology." Indigenous Foundations UBC Arts. <https://indigenousfoundations.arts.ubc.ca/terminology/#firstnations> accessed May 1, 2020.
5. "Genocide." United Nations Office on Genocide Prevention and the Responsibility to Protect. <https://www.un.org/en/genocideprevention/genocide.shtml> accessed February 15, 2020.
6. "Indian." The Canadian Encyclopedia. May 11, 2020. <https://thecanadianencyclopedia.ca/en/article/indian-term> accessed May 15, 2020.
7. The Truth and Reconciliation Commission of Canada. They Came for the Children. Manitoba: Library and Archives Canada Cataloguing in Publication, 2012. pp. 11.
8. "Indian Agents in Canada." The Canadian Encyclopedia. October 25, 2018. <https://www.thecanadianencyclopedia.ca/en/article/indian-agents-in-canada> Accessed May 28, 2020.
9. Webstad, Phyllis. Personal Interview. January. 2020.
10. "Residential School." Truth and Reconciliation Commission. <http://www.trc.ca/about-us.html> accessed October 15, 2020.
11. The Truth and Reconciliation Commission of Canada. They Came for the Children. Manitoba: Library and Archives Canada Cataloguing in Publication, 2012. pp. 5.
12. "Archived - Common Terminology." Indigenous and Northern Affairs Canada. March 11, 2013. <https://www.aadnc-aandc.gc.ca/eng/1358879361384/1358879407462> accessed May 1, 2020.
13. "Intergenerational survivors." Where are the Children. November 28, 2013. <http://wherearethechildren.ca/en/watc_blackboard/intergenerational-survivors/> accessed May 10, 2020.
14. "The Intergenerational Trauma of First Nations Still Run Deep." The Global and Mail. Berube, Kevin. February 16, 2015. <https://www.theglobeandmail.com/life/health-and-fitness/health-advisor/the-intergenerational-trauma-of-first-nations-still-runs-deep/article23013789/> accessed May 24, 2020.
15. "Sir John A Macdonald." The Canadian Encyclopedia. <https://www.thecanadianencyclopedia.ca/en/article/sir-john-alexander-macdonald> accessed on November 30th, 2022
16. "Archived - Common Terminology." Indigenous and Northern Affairs Canada. March 11, 2013. <https://www.aadnc-aandc.gc.ca/eng/1358879361384/1358879407462> accessed May 1, 2020.
17. "Citizenship." Métis National Council. Source quotes R. v. Powley 2003, the Supreme Court of Canada. <https://www.metisnation.ca/about/citizenship>.Accessed November 16, 2022.
18. "National Day for Truth and Reconciliation". Government of Canada. November 15th, 2022. <https://www.canada.ca/en/canadian-heritage/campaigns/national-day-truth-reconciliation.html> Accessed November 22nd, 2022.
19. "On-Reserve First Nations Communities: Canada Pandemic Influenza Preparedness: Planning Guidance for the Health Sector." Government of Canada. December 5, 2017. <https://www.canada.ca/en/public-health/services/flu-influenza/canadian-pandemic-influenza-preparedness-planning-guidance-health-sector/influenza-pandemic-planning-considerations-in-on-reserve-first-nations-communities.html> accessed February 15, 2020.
20. Tarbell, Harold. St. Joseph's Mission Residential School Commemoration Project Document. Remembering, Recovering, and Reconciling. Williams Lake: Tarbell Facilitation Network, 2013.
21. "Residential Schools Findings Point to 'Cultural Genocide,' Commission Chair Says." CBC News. John Paul Tasker. May 15, 2015. <https://www.cbc.ca/news/politics/residential-schools-findings-point-to-cultural-genocide-commission-chair-says-1.3093580> accessed March 30, 2020.
22. "About the National Centre for Truth and Reconciliation." National Centre of Truth and Reconciliation. University of Manitoba. <http://nctr.ca/about-new.php> accessed May 15, 2020.
23. Williams Lake Band. <https://williamslakeband.ca/> accessed April 30, 2020.
24. "Worldview." Oxford Reference. <https://www.oxfordreference.com/view/10.1093/oi/authority.20110803124830471> accessed May 15, 2020.

Grade 9 student Gianna Pellerin's Orange Shirt Day artwork.

Phyllis Webstad on cover photographed by Danielle Shack of DS Photography

Funded by the   Financé par le
Government   gouvernement
of Canada   du Canada   Canada